THE PRE-RAPHAELITE VISION

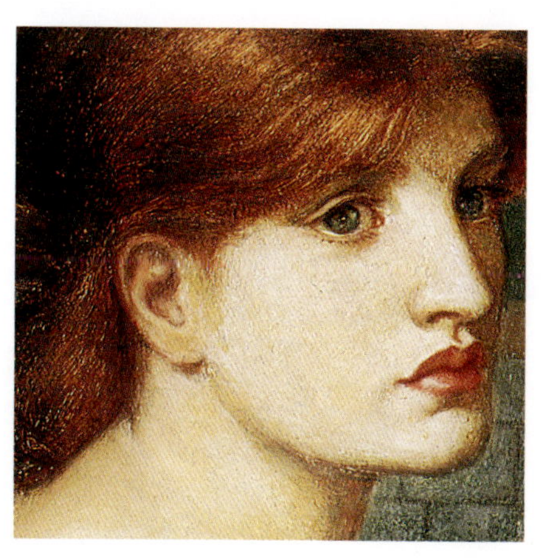

THE BOWER MEADOW
DANTE GABRIEL ROSSETTI
DETAIL AND OVERLEAF

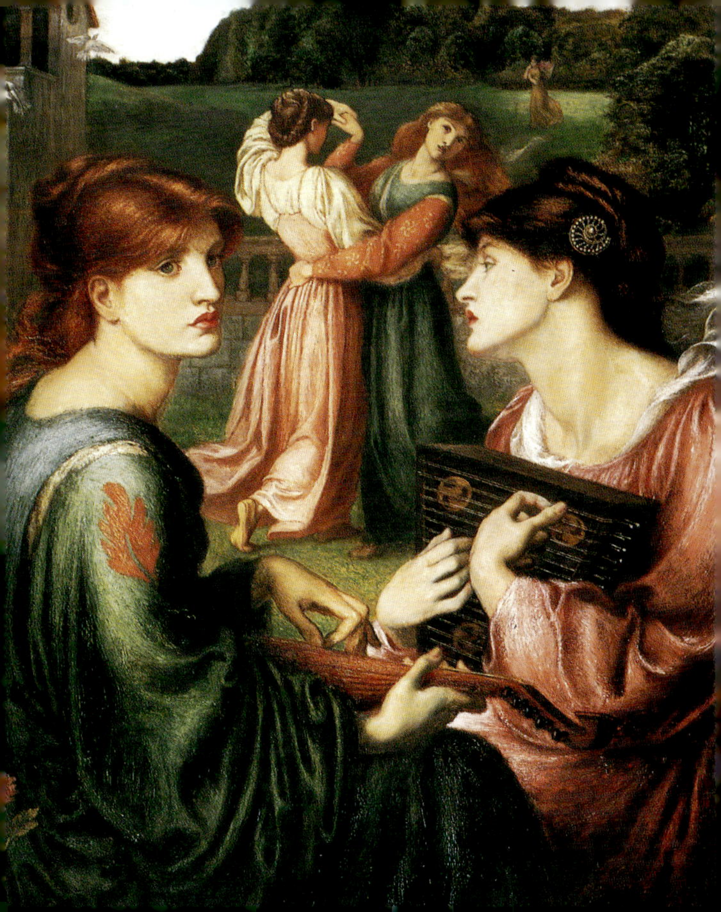

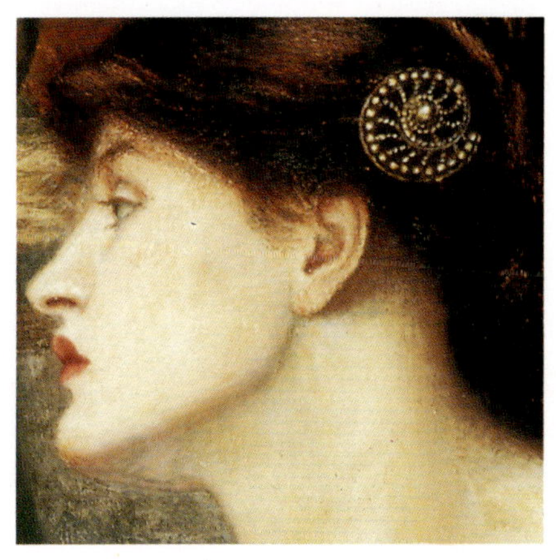

THE PRE-RAPHAELITE VISION

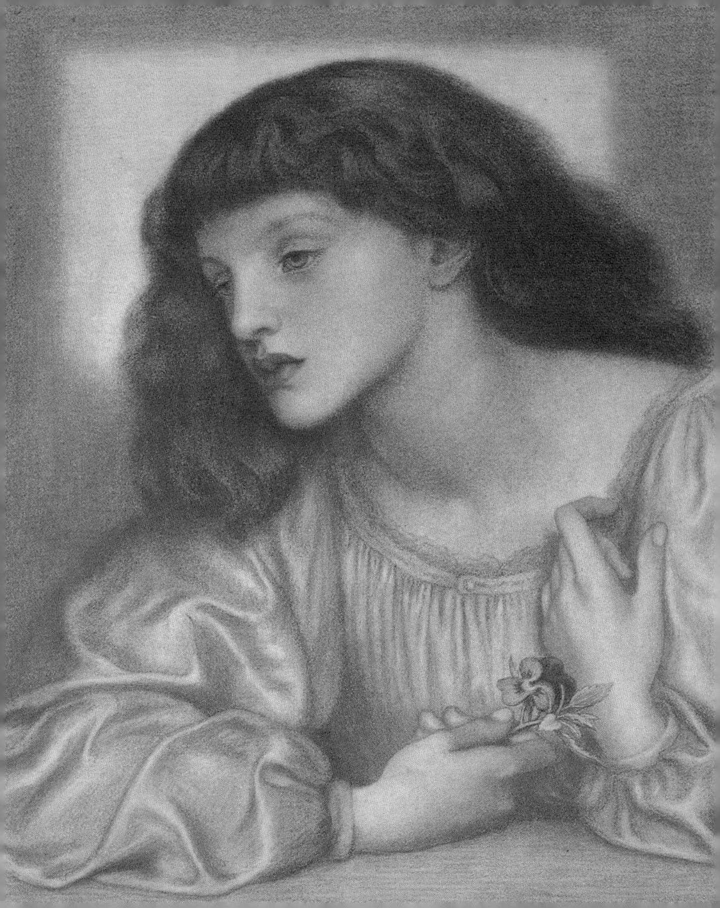

The Pre-Raphaelite Brotherhood was forged in
September 1848 by seven individuals who were
fired by a common enthusiasm for absolute
and uncompromising truth. The Pre-Raphaelite
vision was a late flowering of the Romantic
Movement that had blossomed almost half
a century earlier in the poetry of Byron, Shelley,
Coleridge and Keats. In cultivating a new early
Renaissance taste, the Pre-Raphaelites sought to
deliver painting from the dark ages of gloomy
canvases and from the bondage of academia that
shackled the art of their generation. The founding
members of the Brotherhood – which included the
painters Dante Gabriel Rossetti, William Holman
Hunt and John Everett Millais – were all blessed
with the passion and imagination of youth, which
blazed most brightly in their veneration of female
beauty. This volume represents the Pre-Raphaelite
vision by featuring their portraits of fair women.
Like Jane Burden and Elizabeth Siddal, favourite
models in Rossetti's circle, some were painted
almost obsessively, and with the passing of time
have come to represent an ideal beauty.

MAY MORRIS
DANTE GABRIEL ROSSETTI

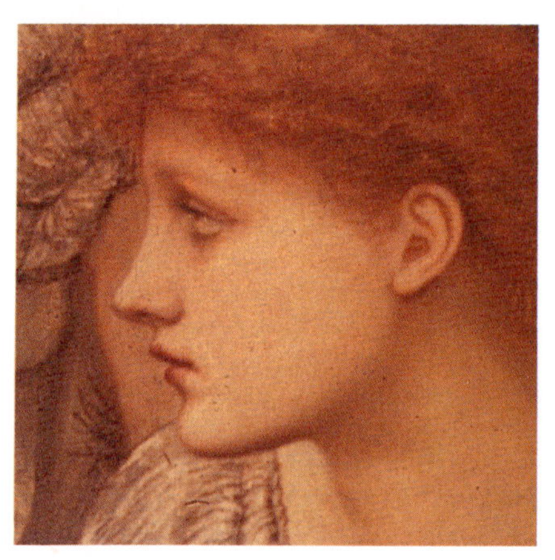

THE GOLDEN STAIRS

EDWARD BURNE-JONES

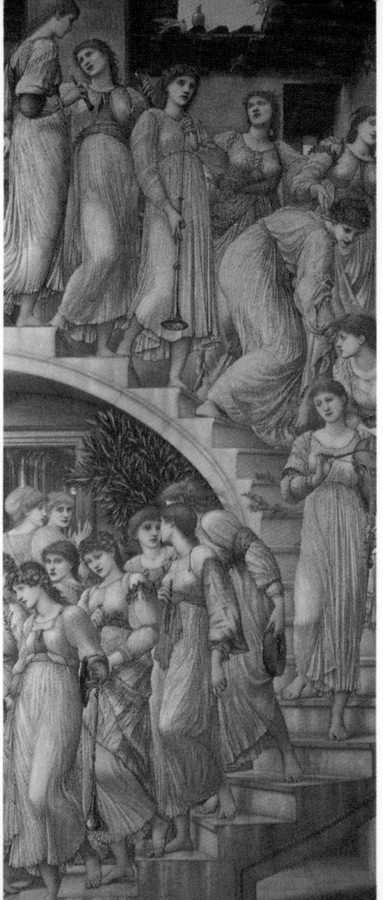

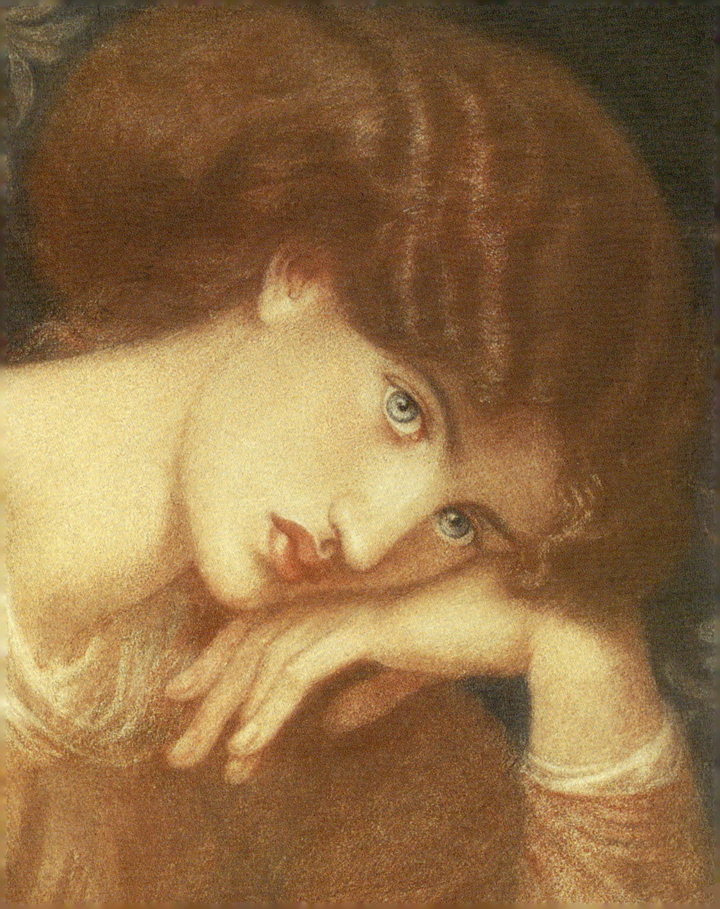

A thing of beauty is a joy for ever:
Its loveliness increases; it will never
Pass into nothingness; but still will keep
A bower quiet for us, and a sleep
Full of sweet dreams, and health, and quiet breathing.

Endymion
(John Keats 1795 -1821)

REVERIE
DANTE GABRIEL ROSSETTI

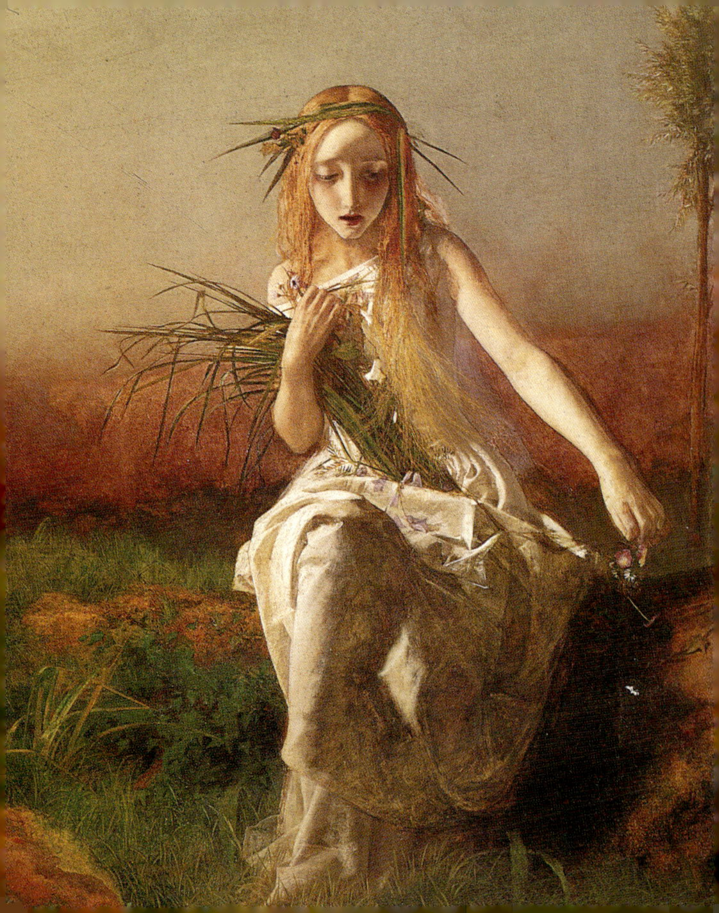

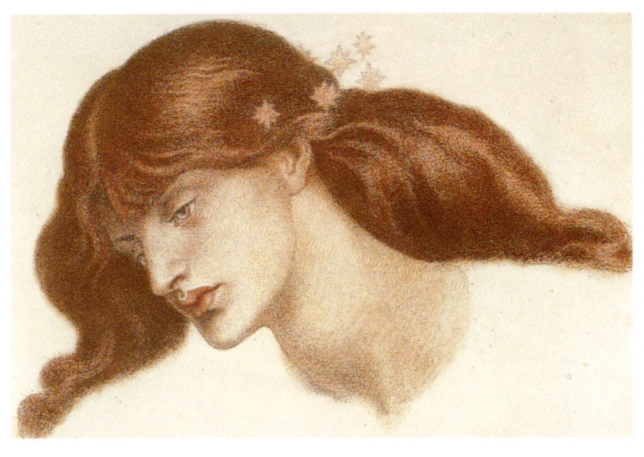

STUDY FOR THE BLESSED DAMOZEL
DANTE GABRIEL ROSSETTI

————————

OPHELIA
ARTHUR HUGHES
DETAIL

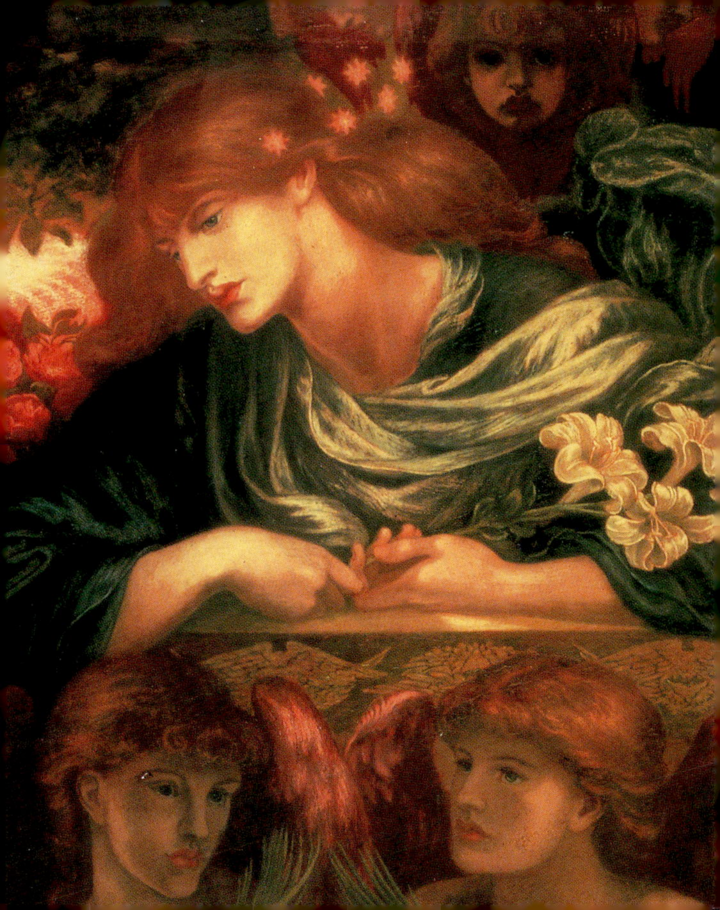

The blessed damozel leaned out
    From the gold bar of Heaven;
Her eyes were deeper than the depth
    Of waters stilled at even;
She had three lilies in her hand,
    And the stars in her hair were seven.

And still she bowed herself and stooped
    Out of the circling charm;
Until her bosom must have made
    The bar she leaned on warm,
And the lilies lay as if asleep
    Along her bended arm.

The Blessed Damozel
(Dante Gabriel Rossetti 1828-82)

THE BLESSED DAMOZEL
DANTE GABRIEL ROSSETTI

PORTRAIT OF MARY SANDYS
FREDERICK SANDYS

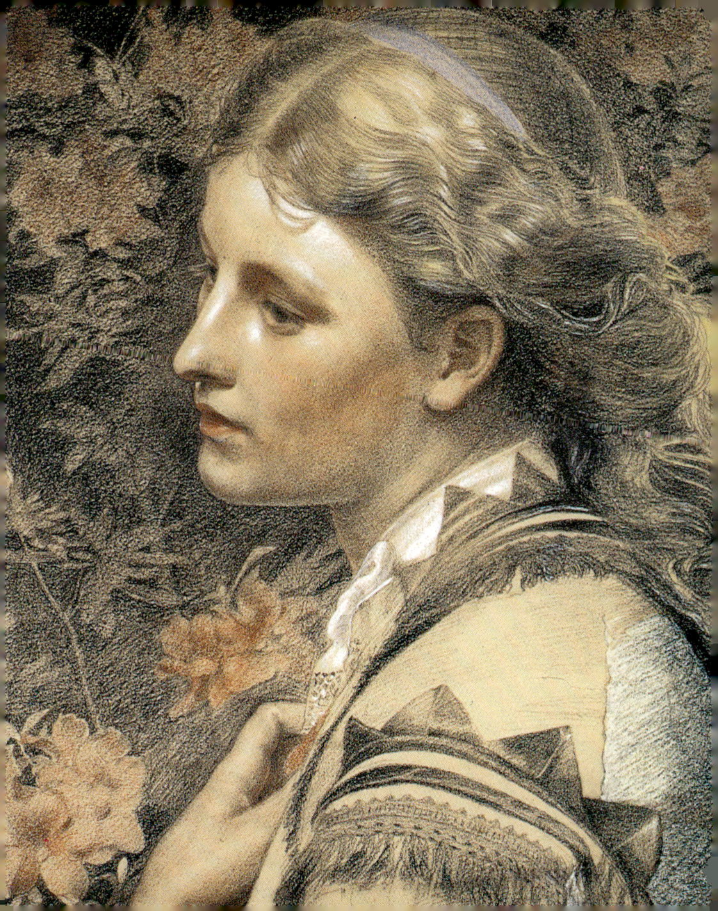

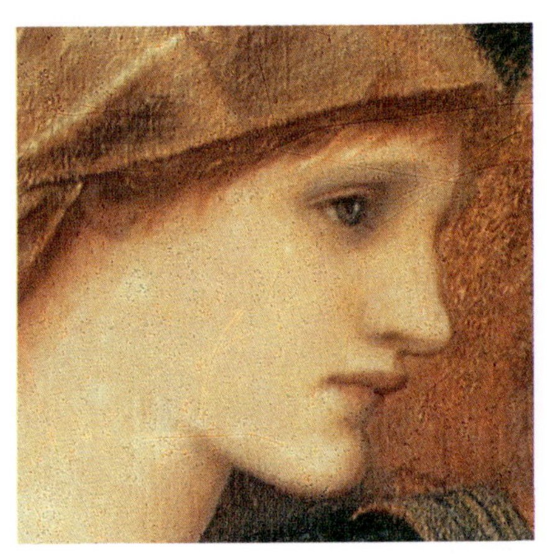

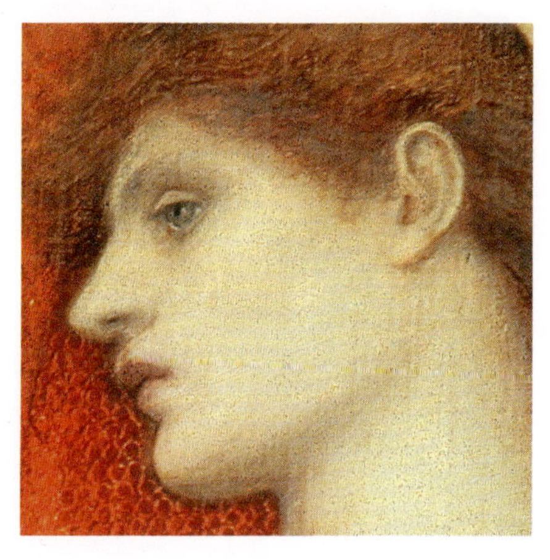

LAUS VENERIS

EDWARD BURNE-JONES

DETAILS AND OVERLEAF

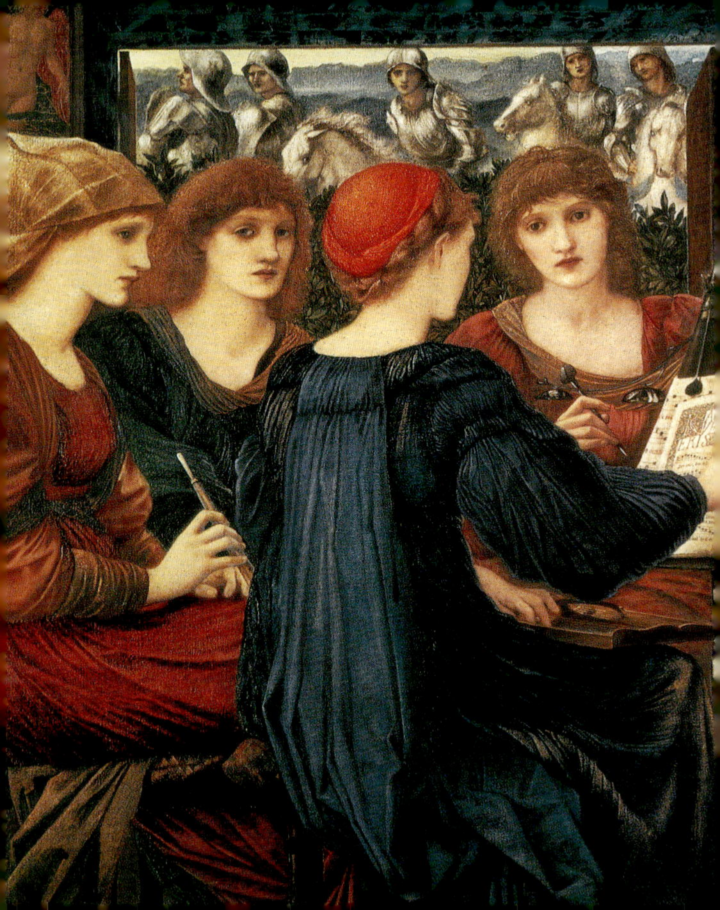

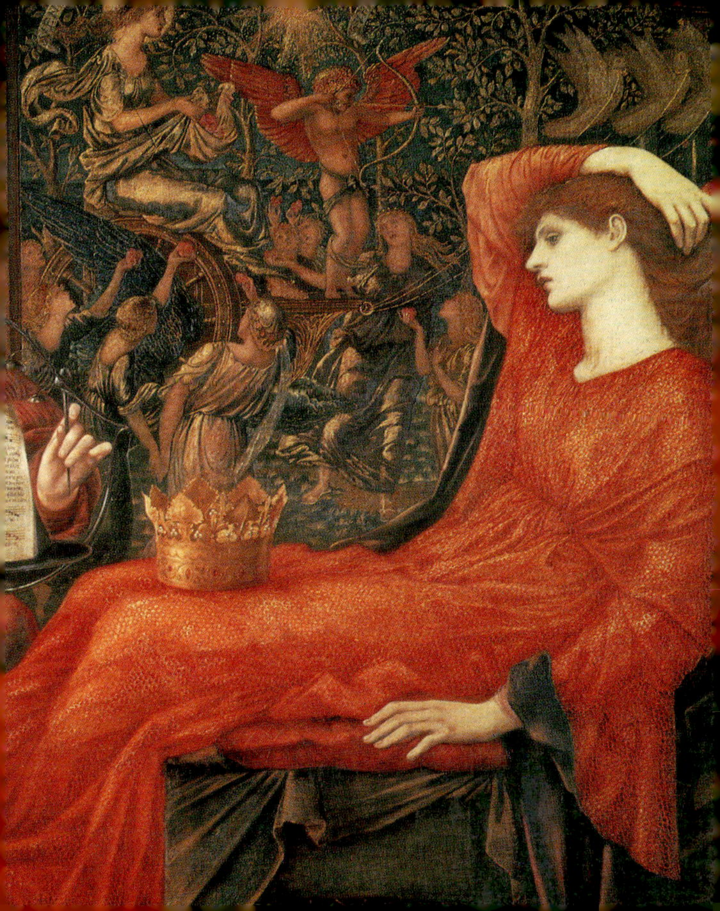

I love my lady; she is very fair;
Her brow is white, and bound by simple hair;
Her spirit sits aloof and high
Although it looks thro' her soft eye
Sweetly and tenderly.

'My Beautiful Lady'
(Thomas Woolner 1825-92)

STUDY OF A GIRL HOLDING A LEAF
DANTE GABRIEL ROSSETTI

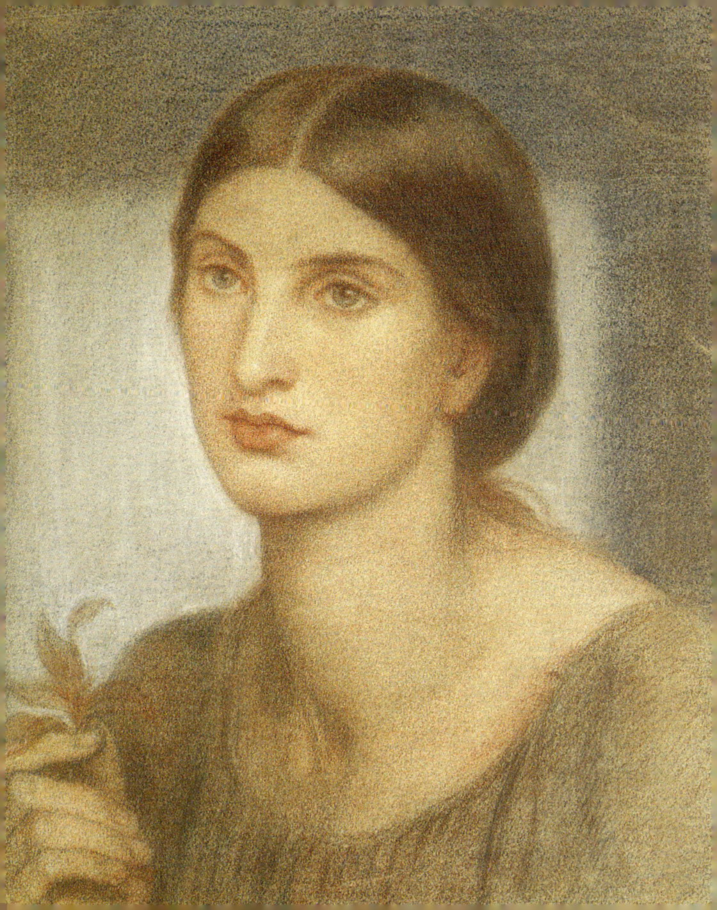

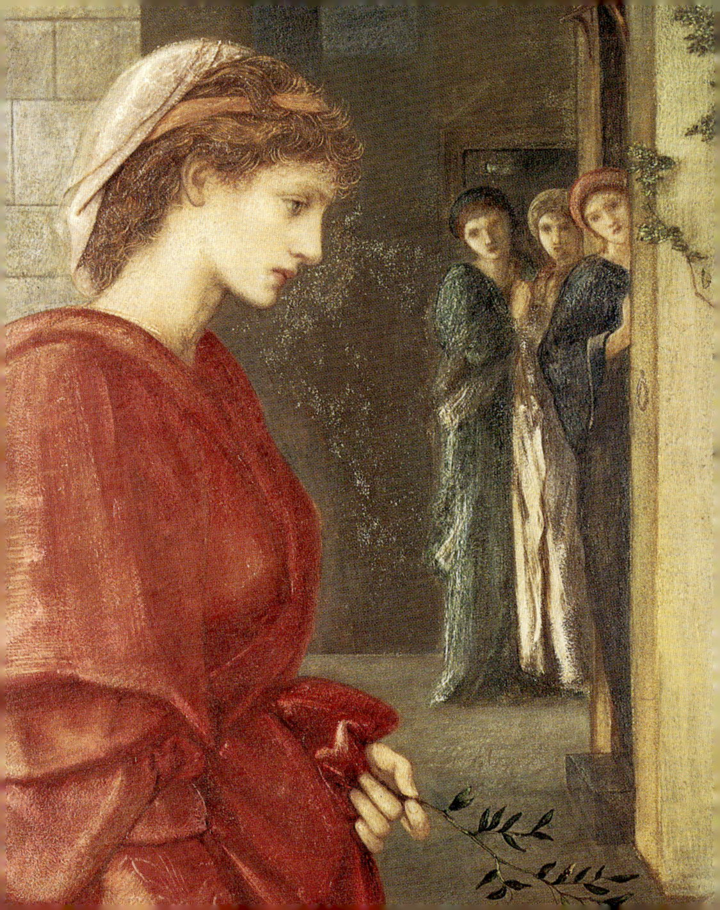

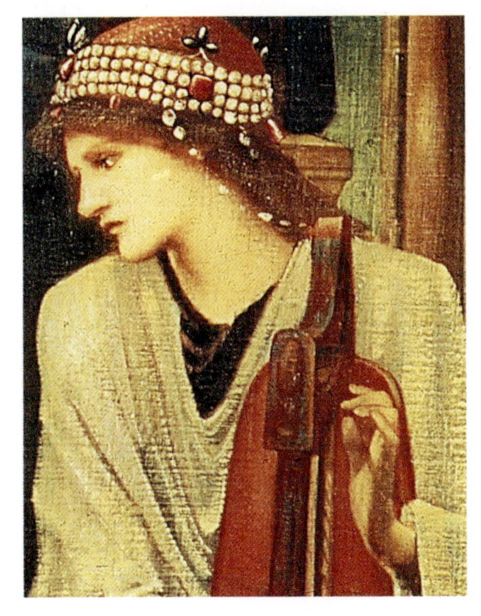

ARTHUR IN AVALON

EDWARD BURNE-JONES

DETAIL

———

BEATRICE FROM DANTE'S 'DIVINE COMEDY'

EDWARD BURNE-JONES

IL DOLCE FAR NIENTE
WILLIAM HOLMAN HUNT

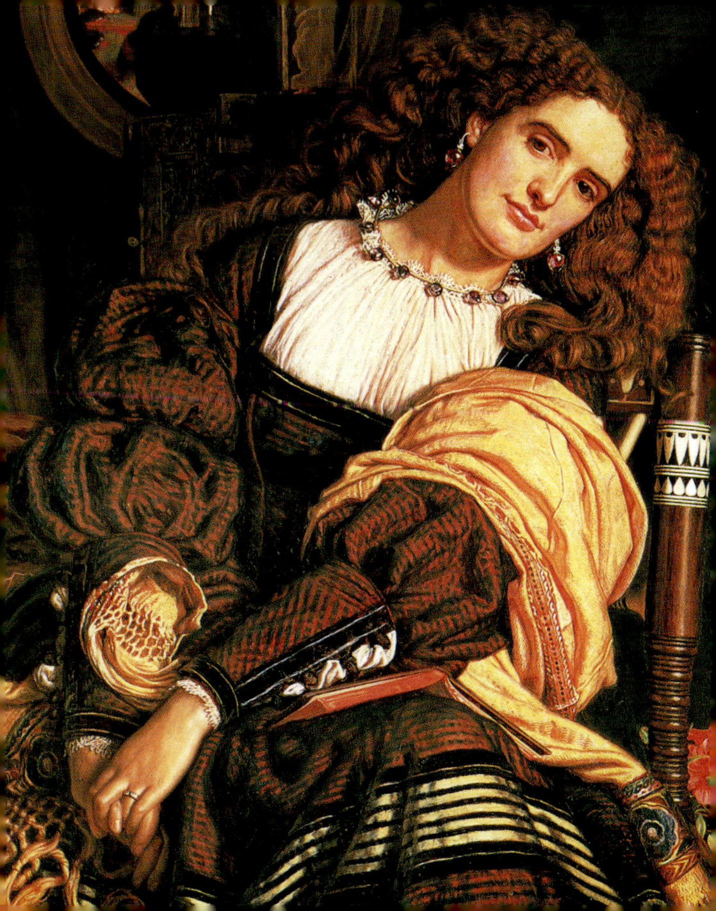

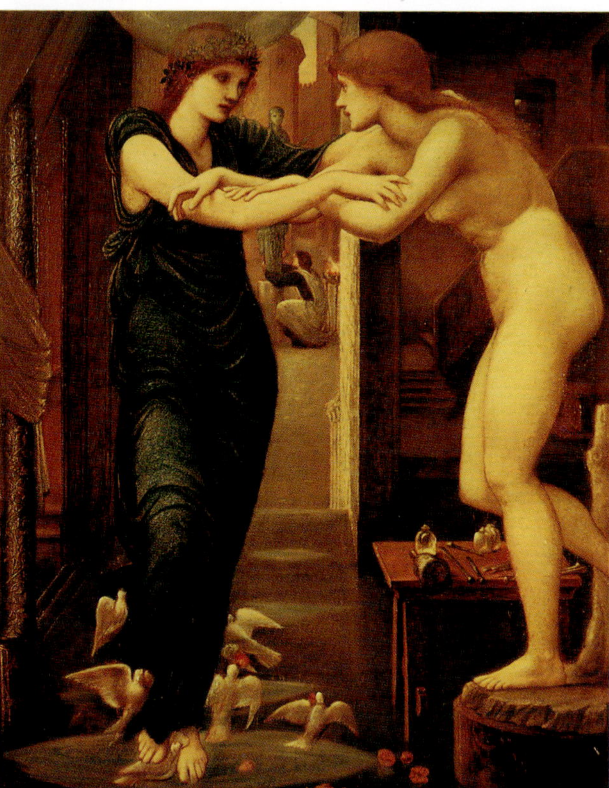

Your gown going off, such beautious state reveals,
As when from flowry meads th'hills shadowe steales...
Full nakedness! All joyes are due to thee,
As souls unbodied, bodies uncloth'd must be.

To His Mistress on Going to Bed
(John Donne 1572-1631)

THE GODHEAD FIRES
EDWARD BURNE-JONES

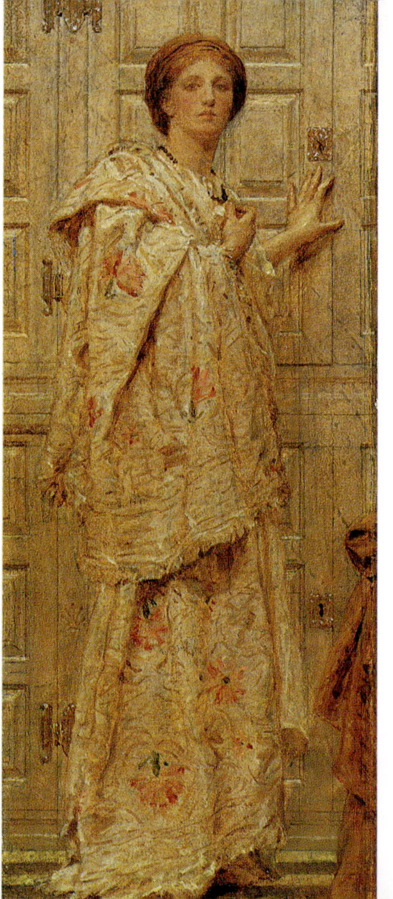

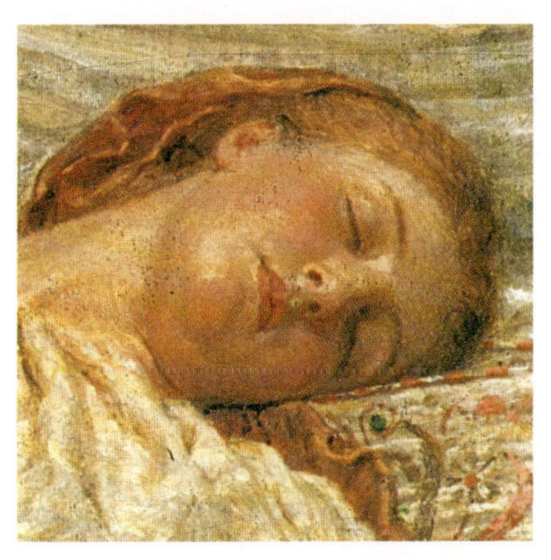

DREAMERS
ALBERT JOSEPH MOORE
DETAIL AND OVERLEAF

———

AN EMBROIDERY
ALBERT JOSEPH MOORE

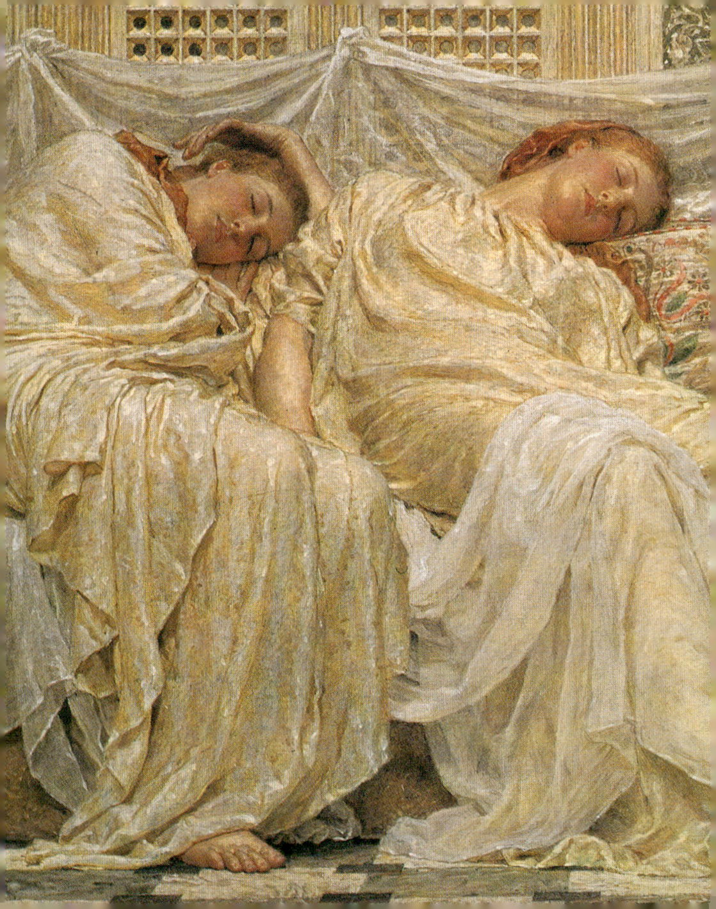

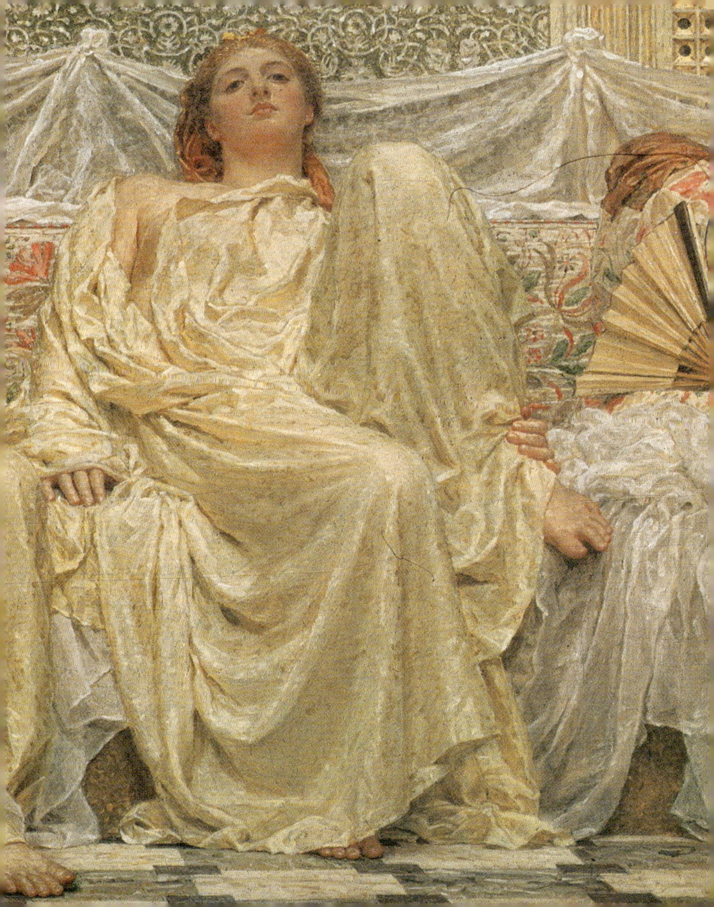

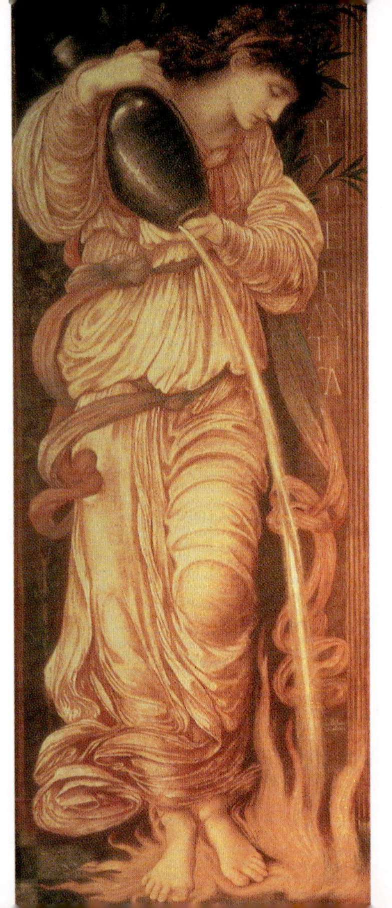

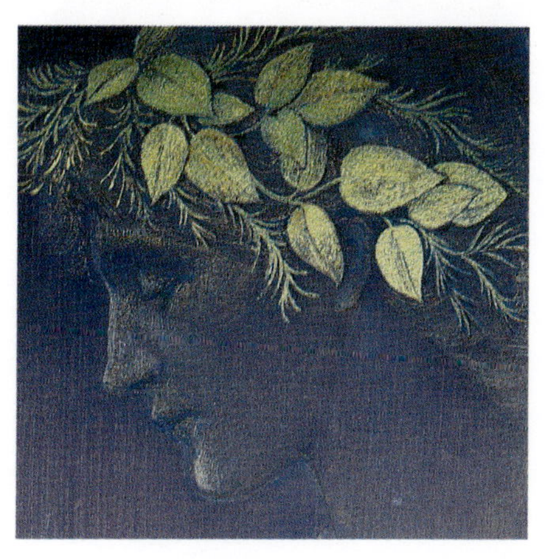

GIRL'S HEAD

EDWARD BURNE-JONES

———

TEMPERANTIA

EDWARD BURNE-JONES

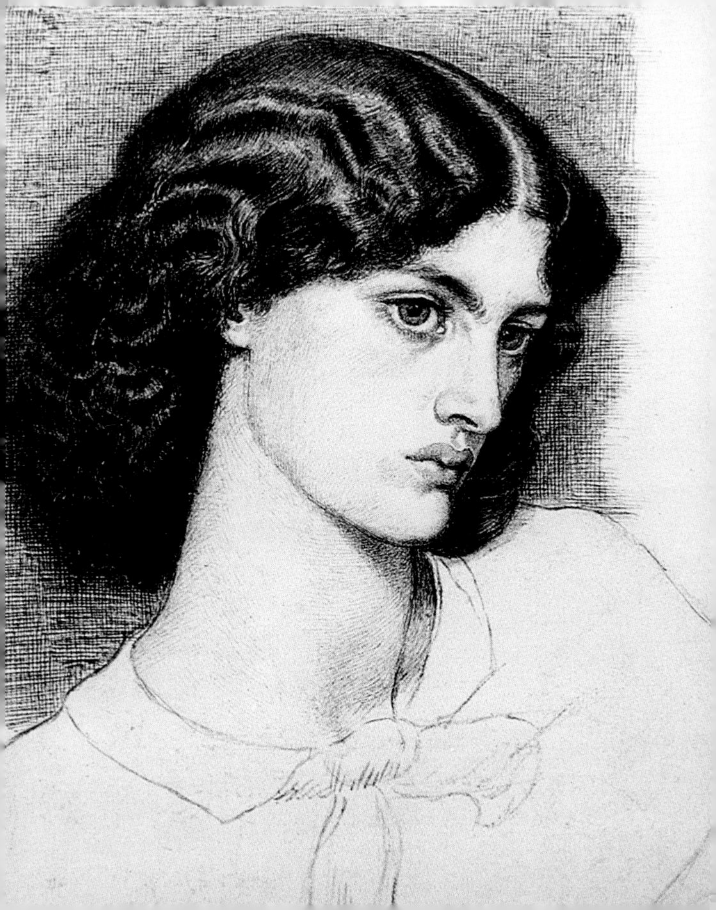

An hundred years should go to praise
Thine Eyes and on thy Forehead Gaze.
Two hundred to adore each Breast:
But thirty thousand to the rest
An Age at least to every part,
And the last Age should show your Heart.
For Lady you deserve this State;
Nor would I love at lower rate.

To His Coy Mistress
(Andrew Marvell 1621-78)

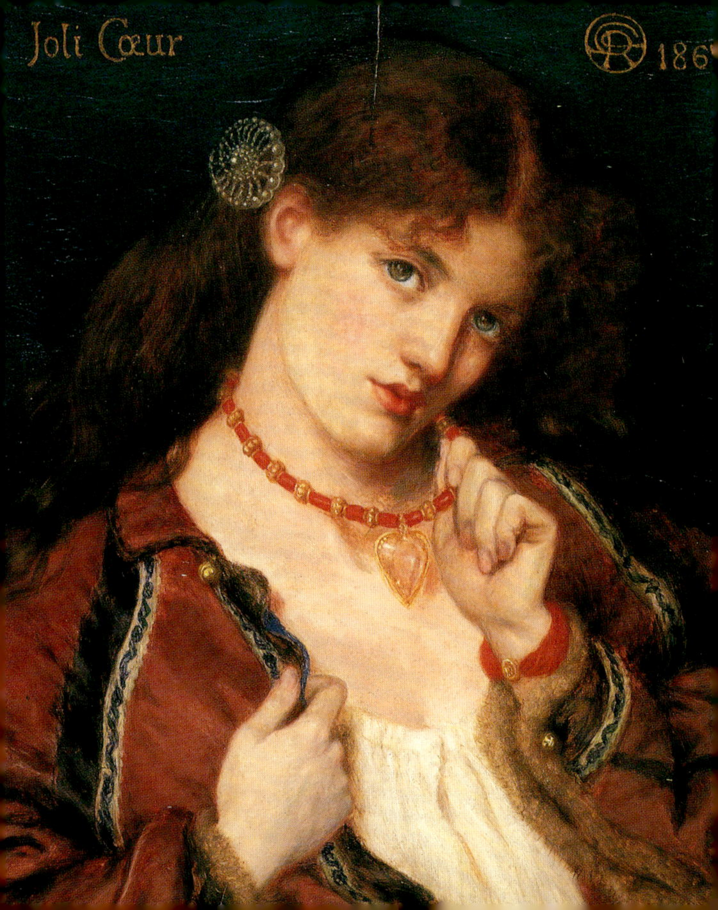

Joli Cœur
186

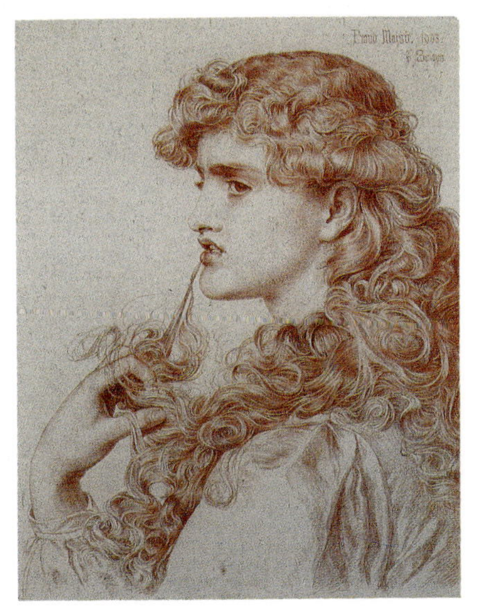

PROUD MAISIE

FREDERICK SANDYS

———

JOLI COEUR

DANTE GABRIEL ROSSETTI

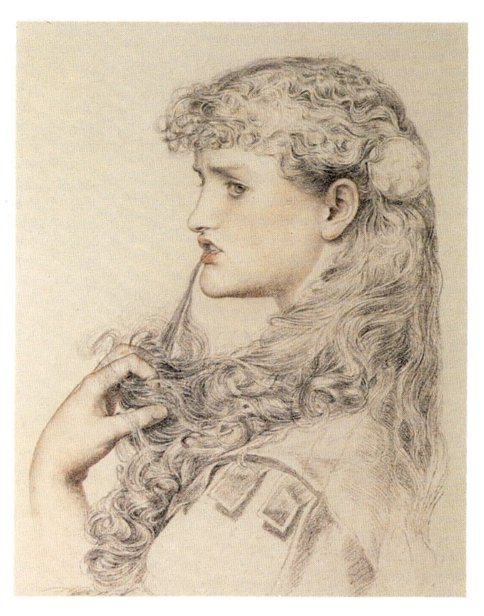

PROUD MAISIE

FREDERICK SANDYS

—

LOVE'S SHADOW

FREDERICK SANDYS

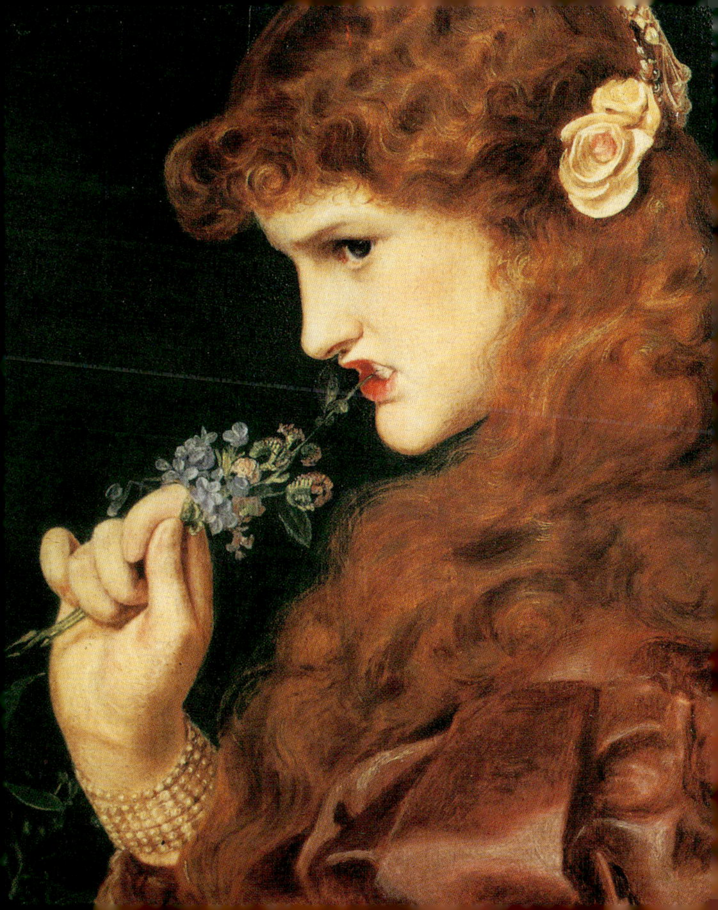

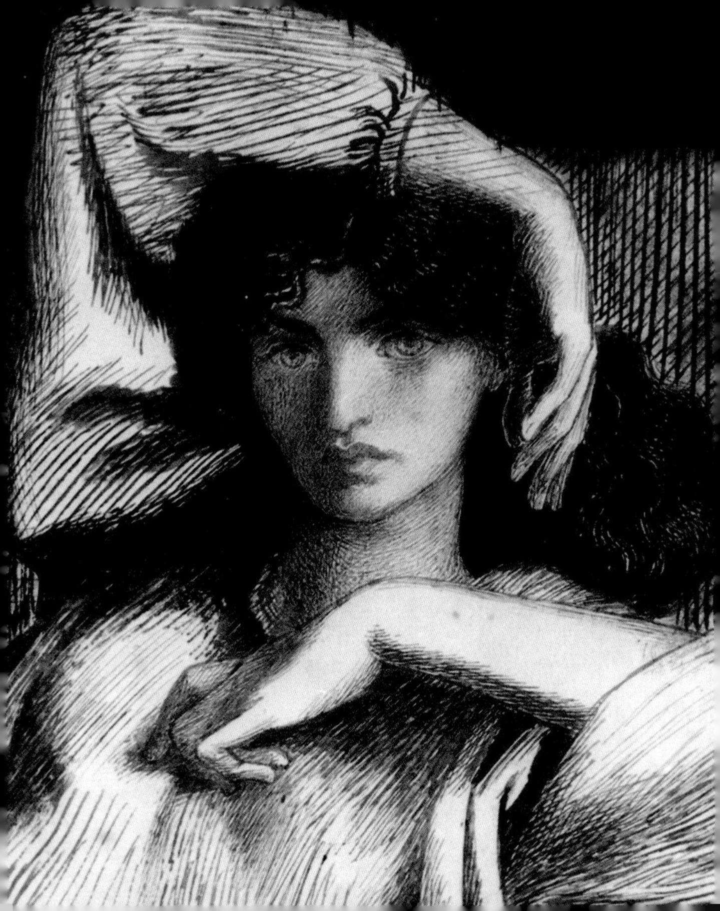

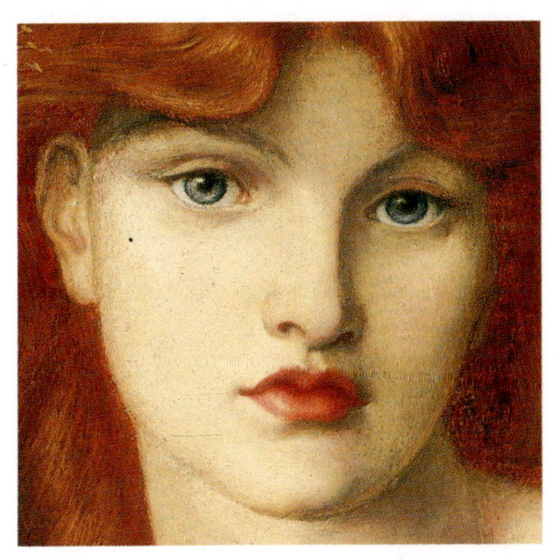

LA GHIRLANDATA
DANTE GABRIEL ROSSETTI
DETAIL AND OVERLEAF

———

MRS WILLIAM MORRIS
DANTE GABRIEL ROSSETTI

There is a garden in her face,
  Where roses and white lilies grow;
A heavenly paradise is that place,
  Wherein all pleasant fruits do flow.

Cherry-Ripe
(Thomas Campion 1567-1620)

LA GHIRLANDATA
DANTE GABRIEL ROSSETTI

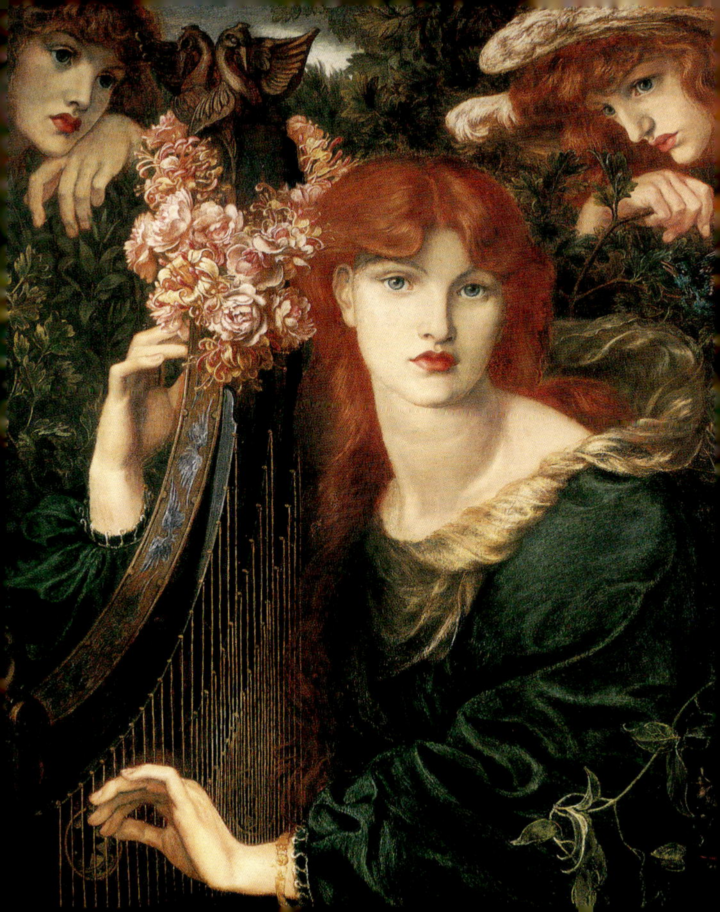

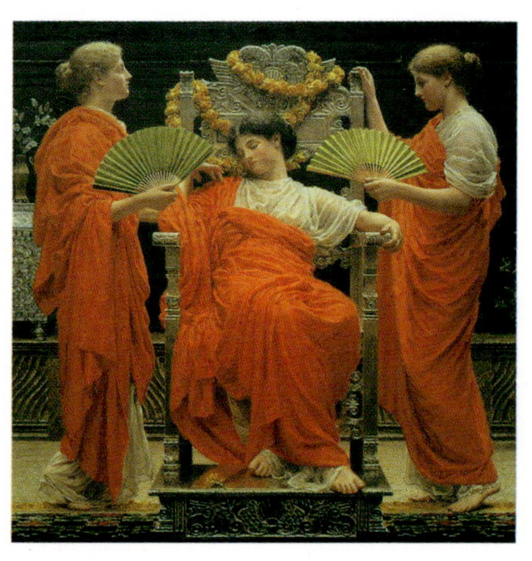

MIDSUMMER

ALBERT JOSEPH MOORE

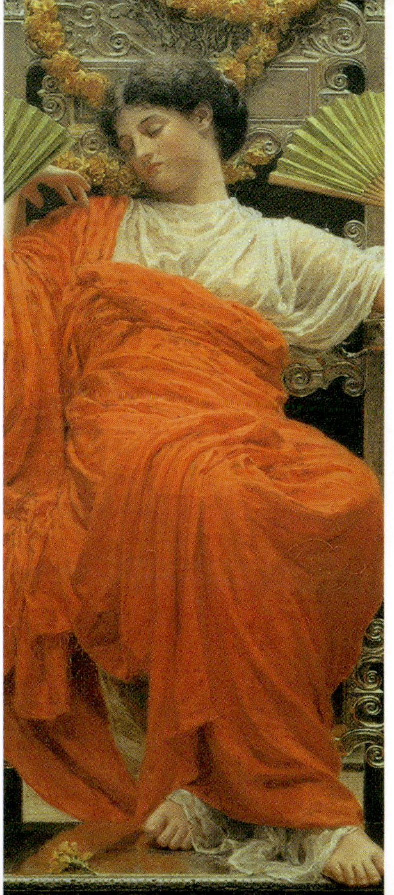

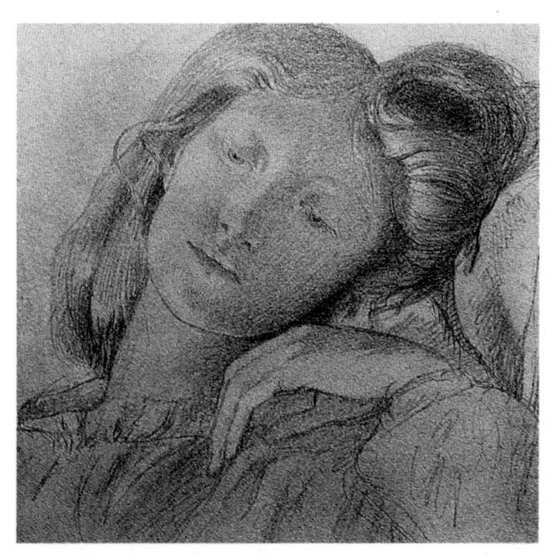

THE ARTIST'S WIFE
DANTE GABRIEL ROSSETTI

———

VIVIEN
FREDERICK SANDYS

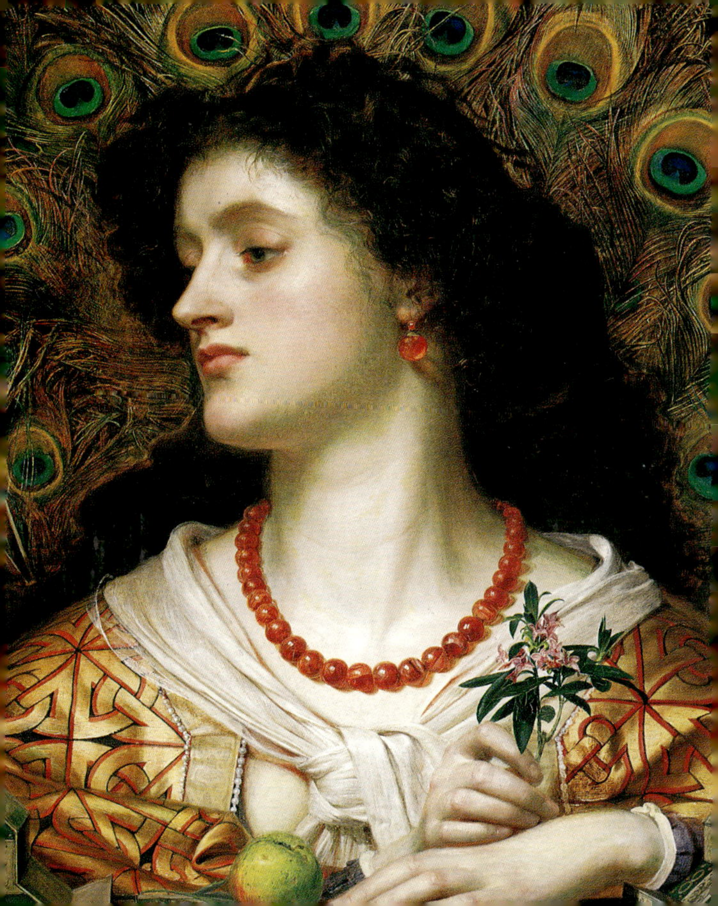

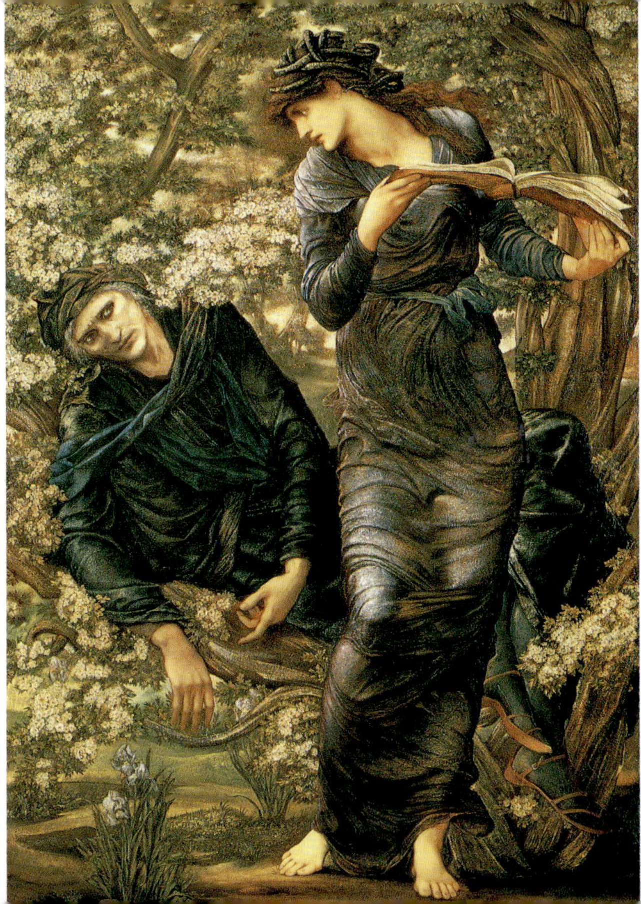

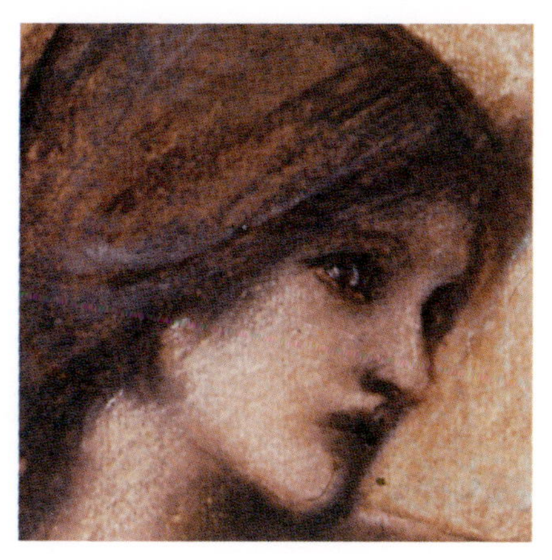

THE THREE GRACES
EDWARD BURNE-JONES
DETAIL AND OVERLEAF

———————

THE BEGUILING OF MERLIN
EDWARD BURNE-JONES

Those were the Graces, daughters of delight,
   Handmaides of Venus, which are wont to haunt
Uppon this hill, and daunce there day and night:
   Those three to men all gifts of grace do graunt,

The Faerie Queene
(Edmund Spenser 1552?-99)

THE THREE GRACES
EDWARD BURNE-JONES

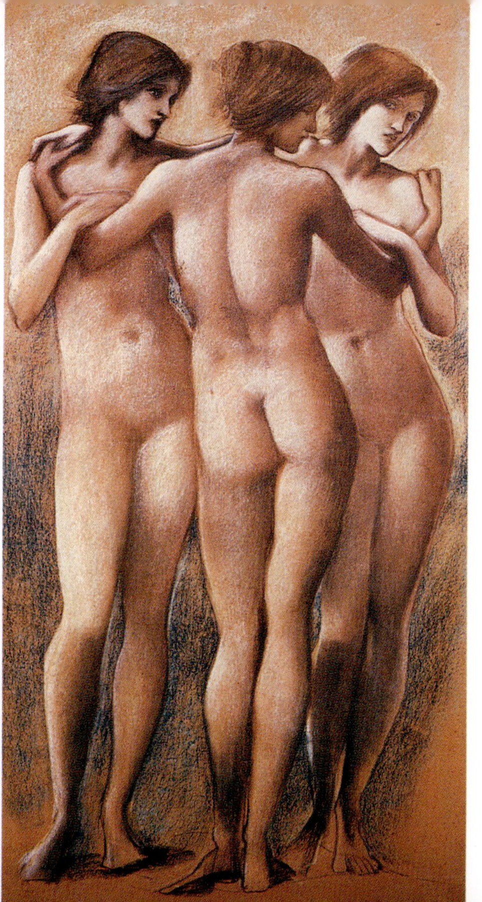

‘YES OR NO?’
JOHN EVERETT MILLAIS

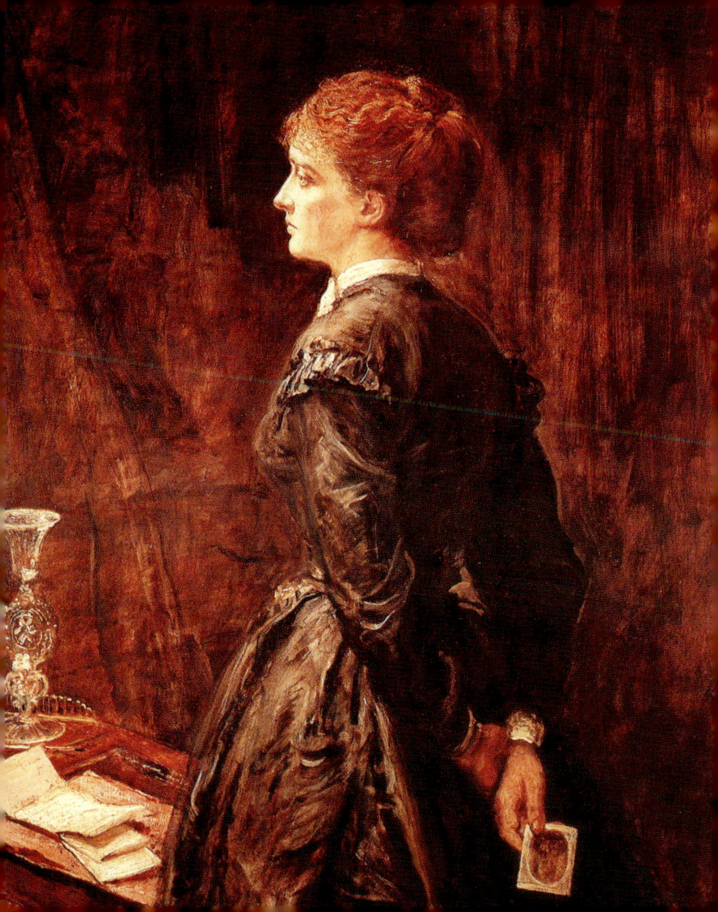

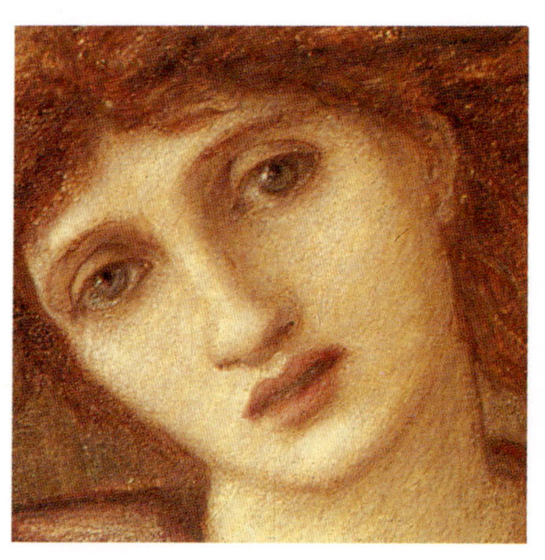

GARDEN OF THE HESPERIDES

EDWARD BURNE-JONES

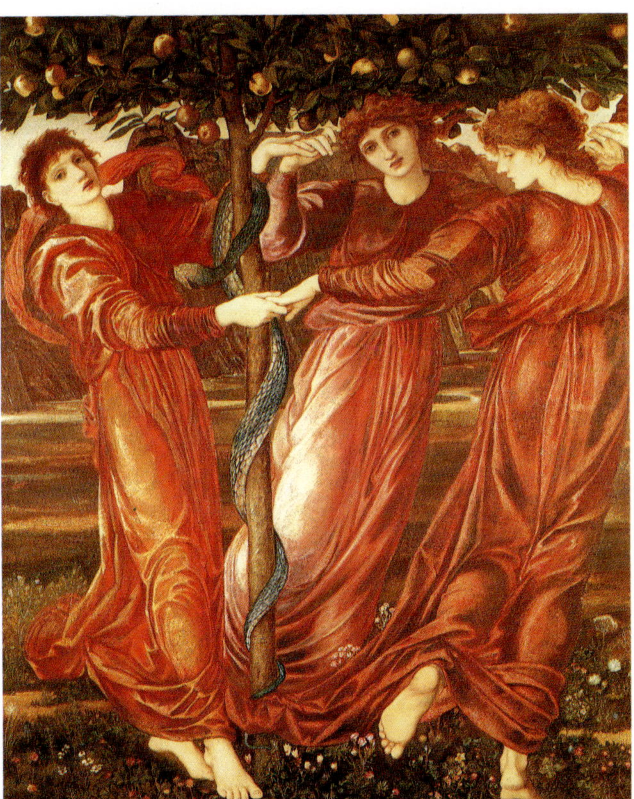

Beauty is Nature's coin, must not be hoarded,
But must be current, and the good thereof
Consists in mutual and partaken bliss,
Unsavory in th'enjoyment of itself.
If you let slip time, like a neglected rose
It withers on the stalk with languished head.
Beauty is Nature's brag, and must be shown

Comus
(John Milton 1608-74)

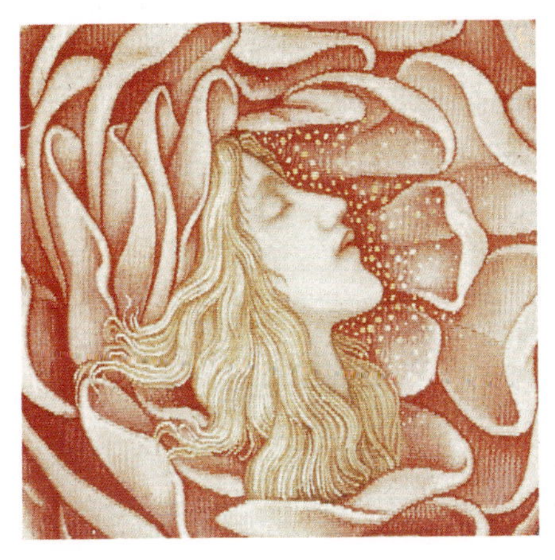

THE HEART OF THE ROSE
EDWARD BURNE-JONES
DETAIL AND OVERLEAF

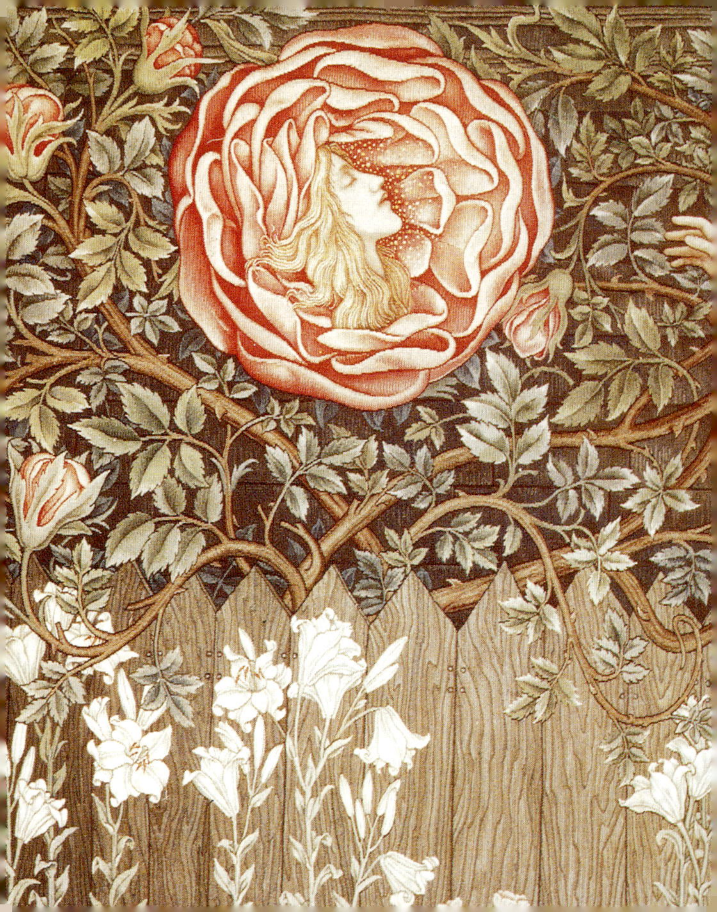

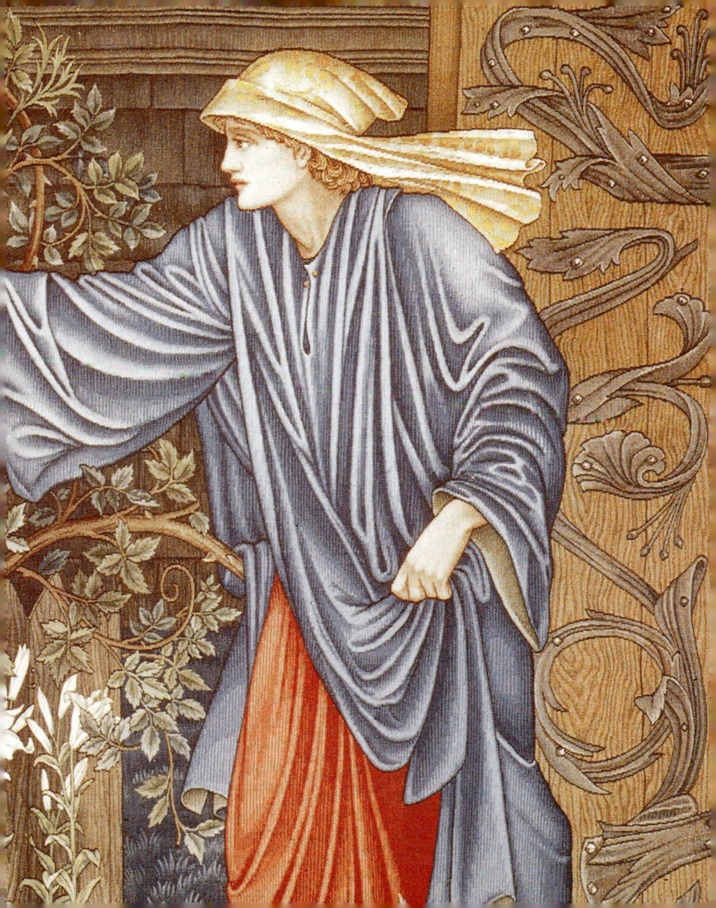

PORTRAIT OF A LADY
DANTE GABRIEL ROSSETTI

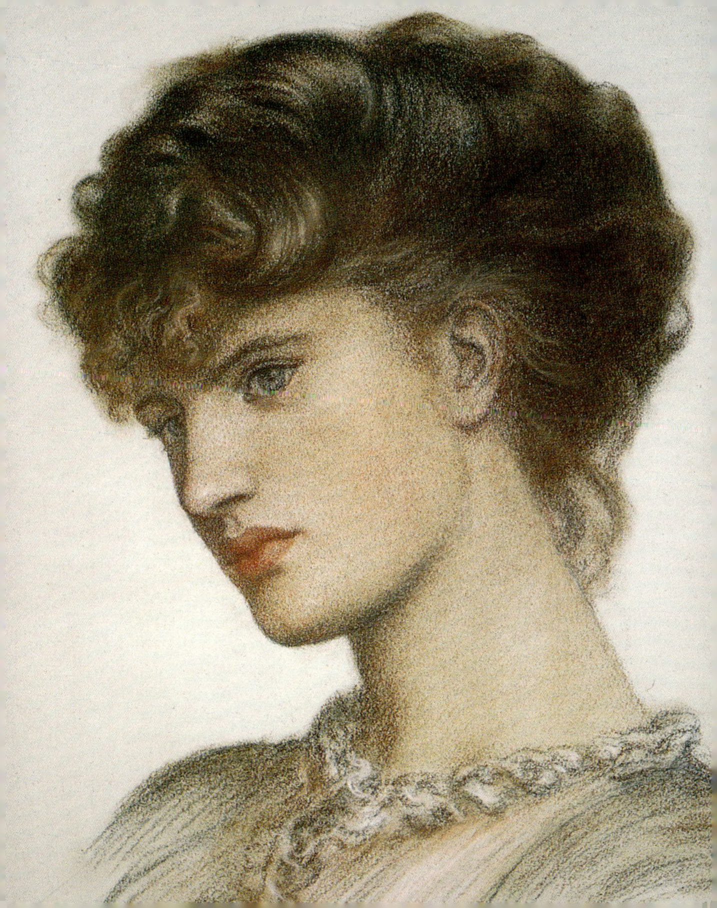

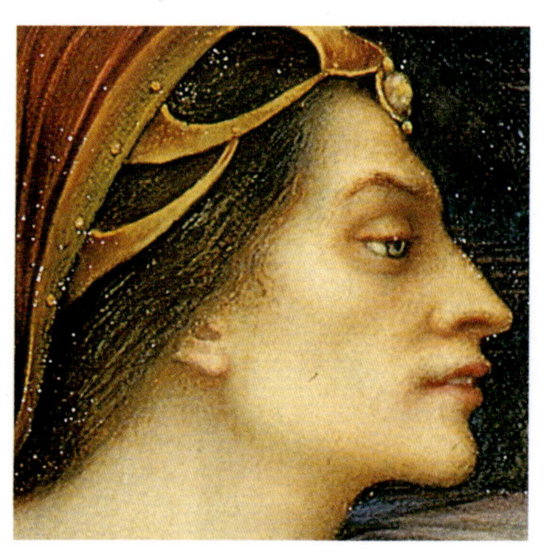

QUEEN ELEANOR AND FAIR ROSAMUND
EVELYN DE MORGAN

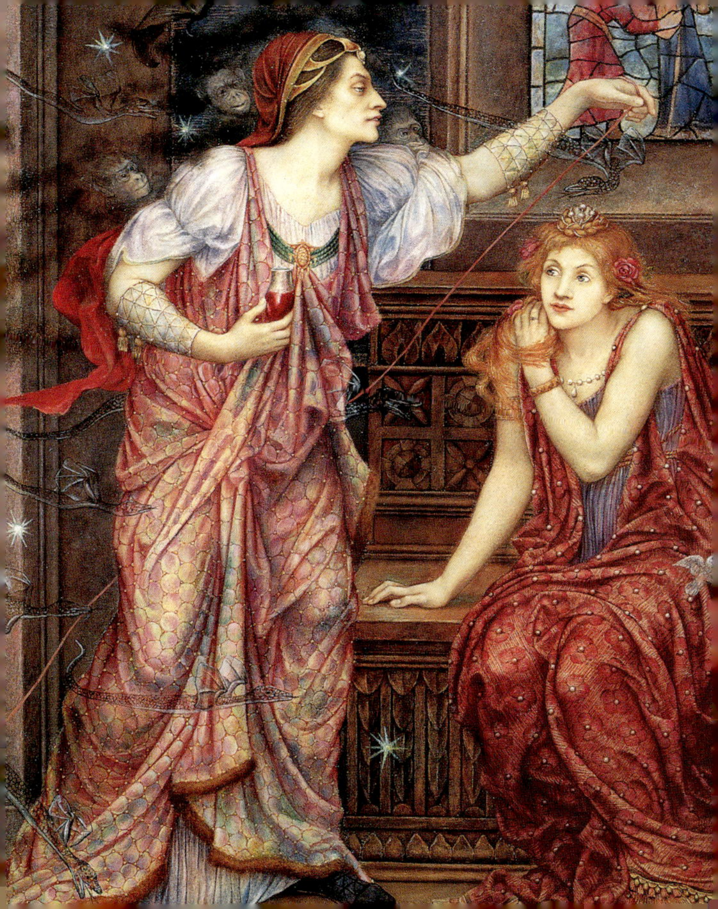

ANNIE MILLER
DANTE GABRIEL ROSSETTI

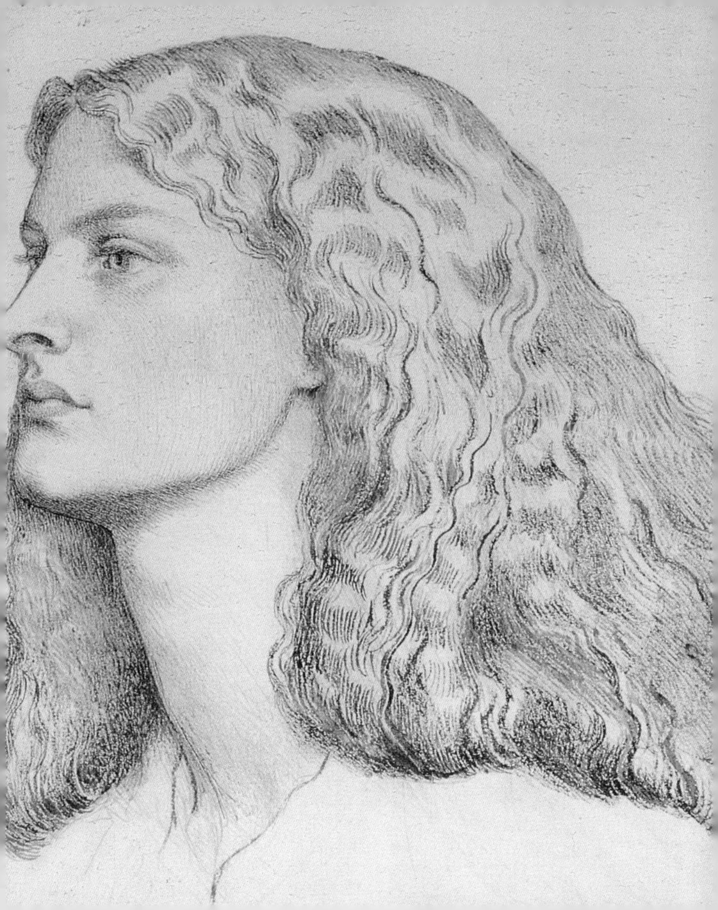

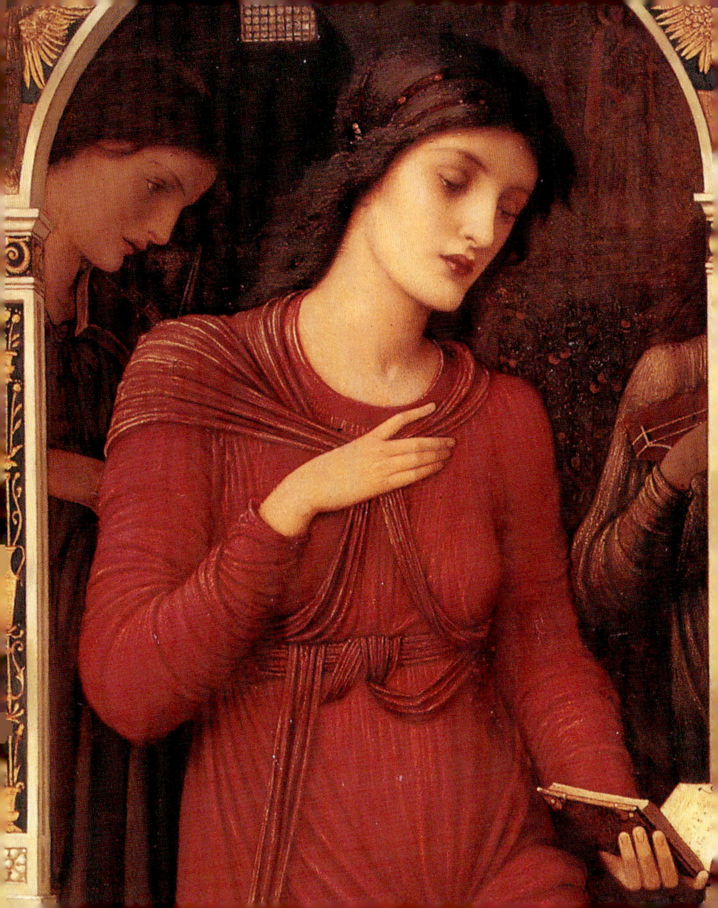

Lady, there's fragrance in your sighs,
And sunlight in your glances;
I never saw such lips and eyes
In pictures or romances;
And Love will readily suppose,
To make you quite enslaving,
That you have taste for verse and prose,
Hot pressed, and line engraving.

Lines written for a blank page
of 'The Keepsake'
(W. M. Praed 1802-39)

A SYMPHONY
JOHN MELHUISH STRUDWICK
DETAIL

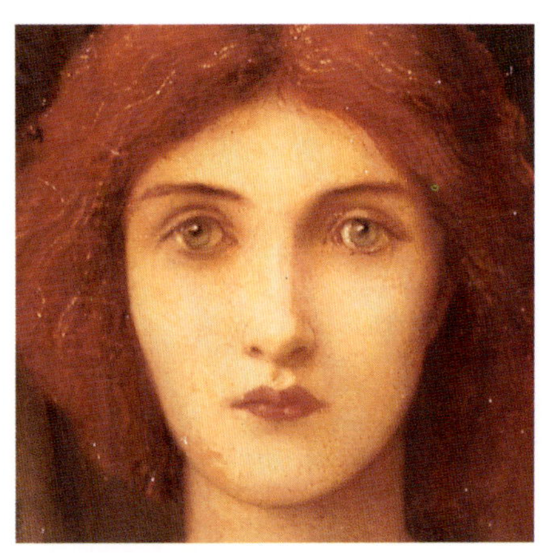

A SYMPHONY

JOHN MELHUISH STRUDWICK

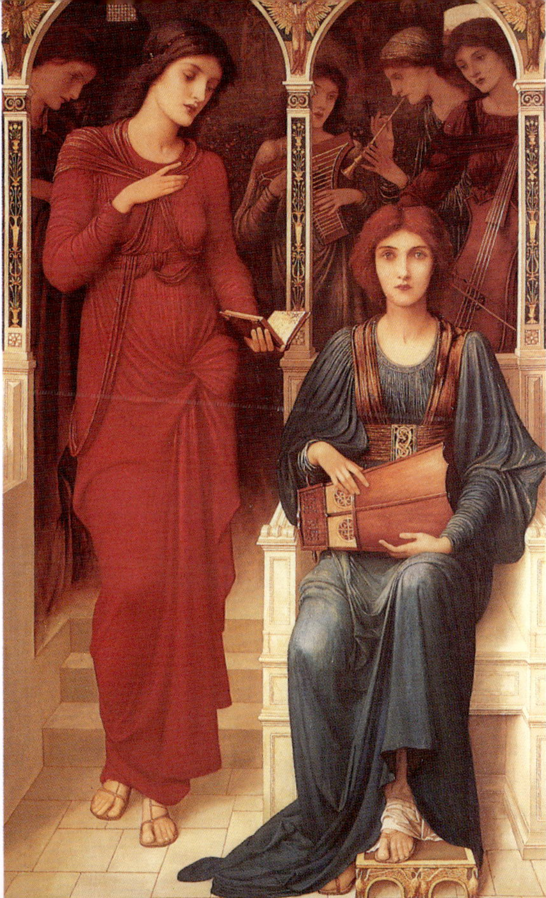

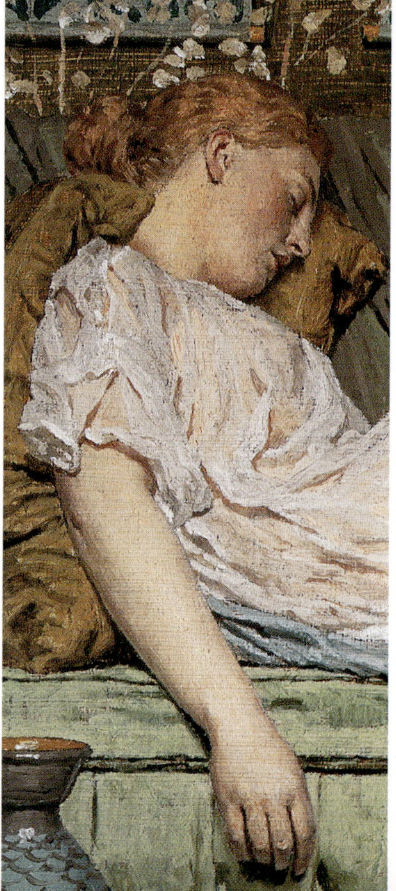

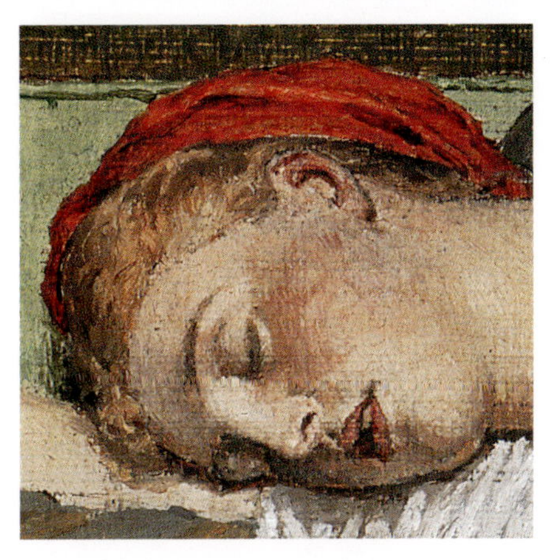

APPLES
ALBERT JOSEPH MOORE
DETAILS AND OVERLEAF

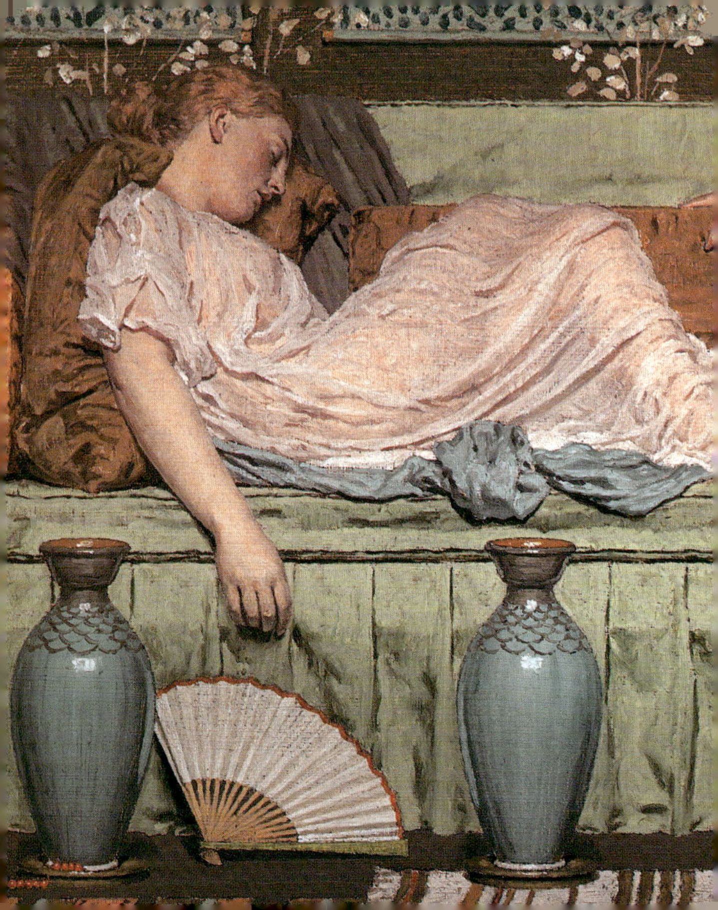

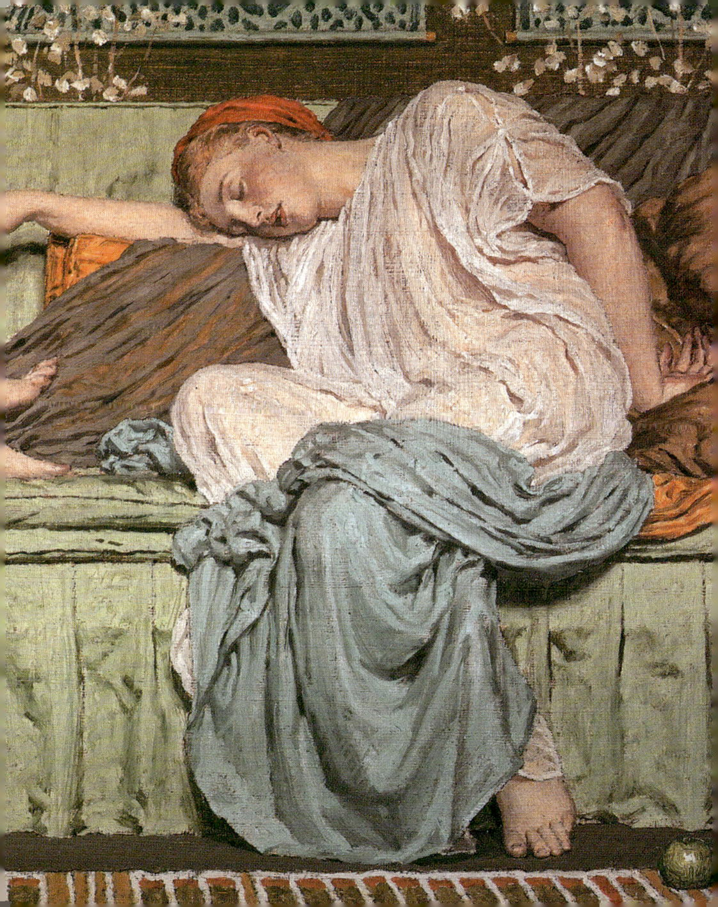

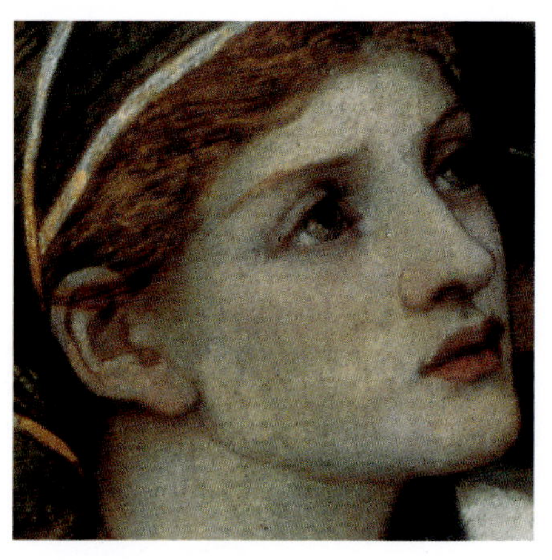

LOVE AND THE MAIDEN
SPENCER STANHOPE
DETAIL AND OVERLEAF

Light feet, dark violet eyes, and parted hair,
Soft dimpled hands, white neck, and creamy breast,
Are things on which the dazzled senses rest
Till the fond, fixèd eyes, forget they stare.

'Woman! when I behold thee'
(John Keats 1795-1821)

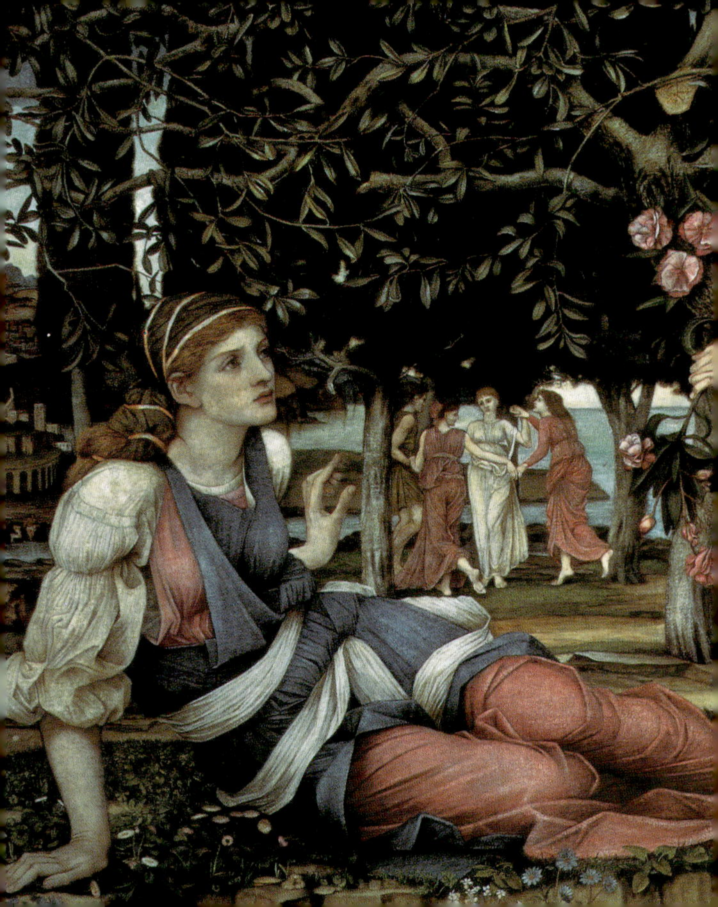

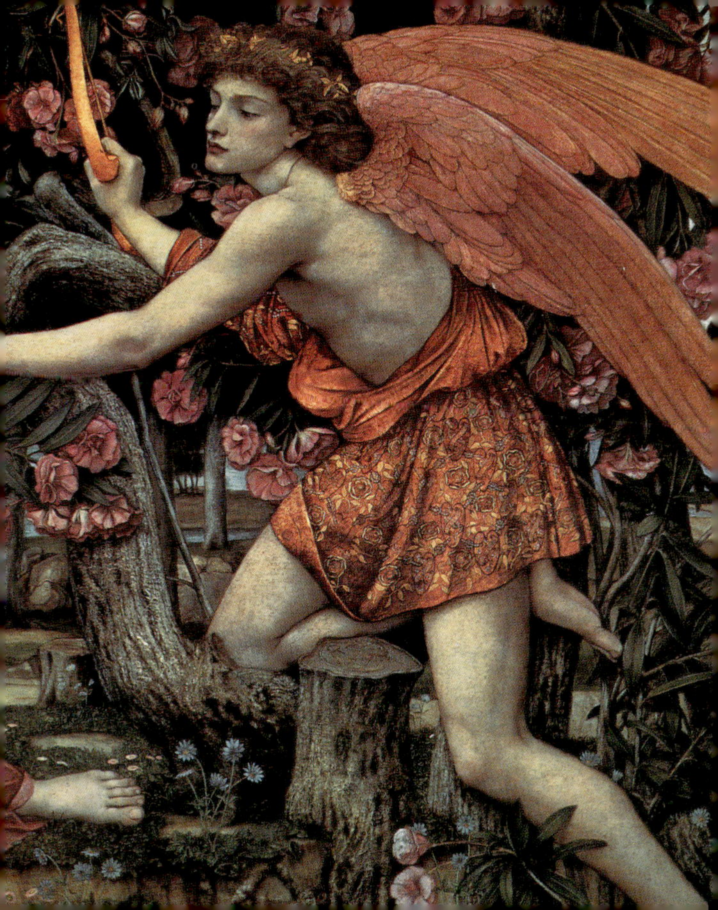

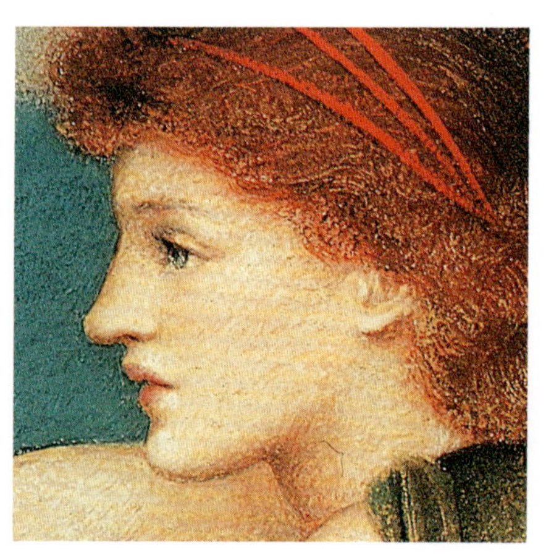

HERO AWAITING THE RETURN OF LEANDER
EVELYN DE MORGAN

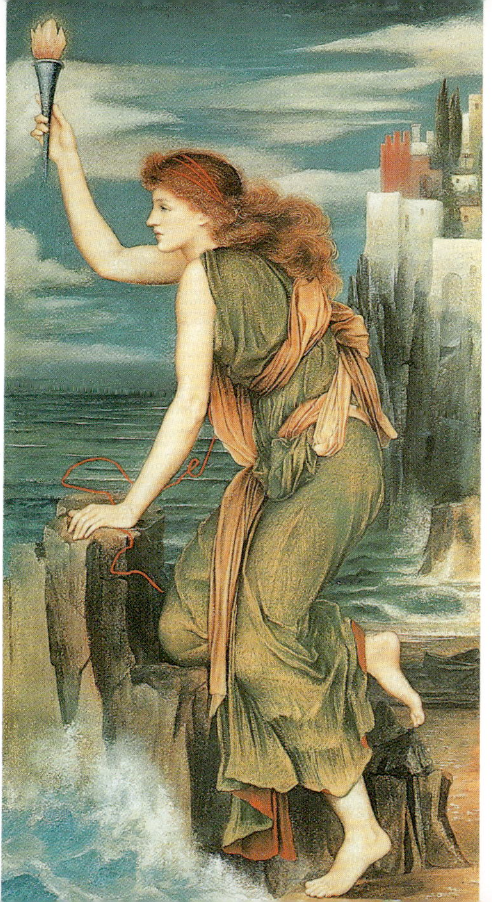

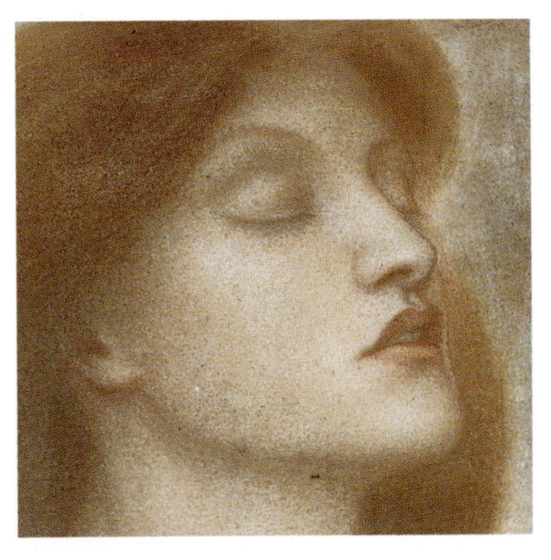

BEATA BEATRIX

DANTE GABRIEL ROSSETTI

DETAIL

———

LA DONNA DELLA FIAMMA

DANTE GABRIEL ROSSETTI

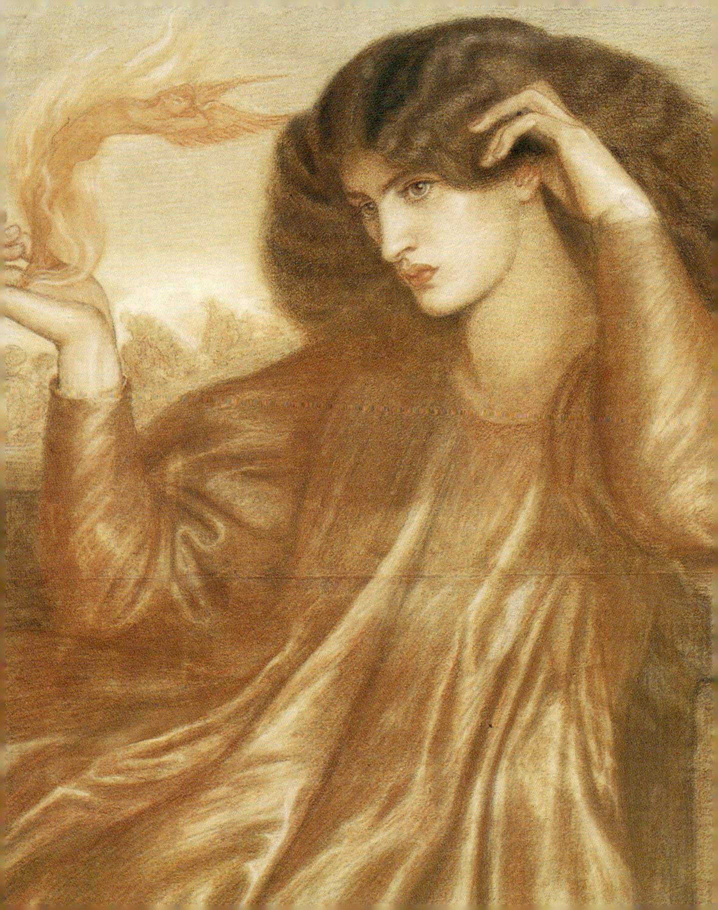

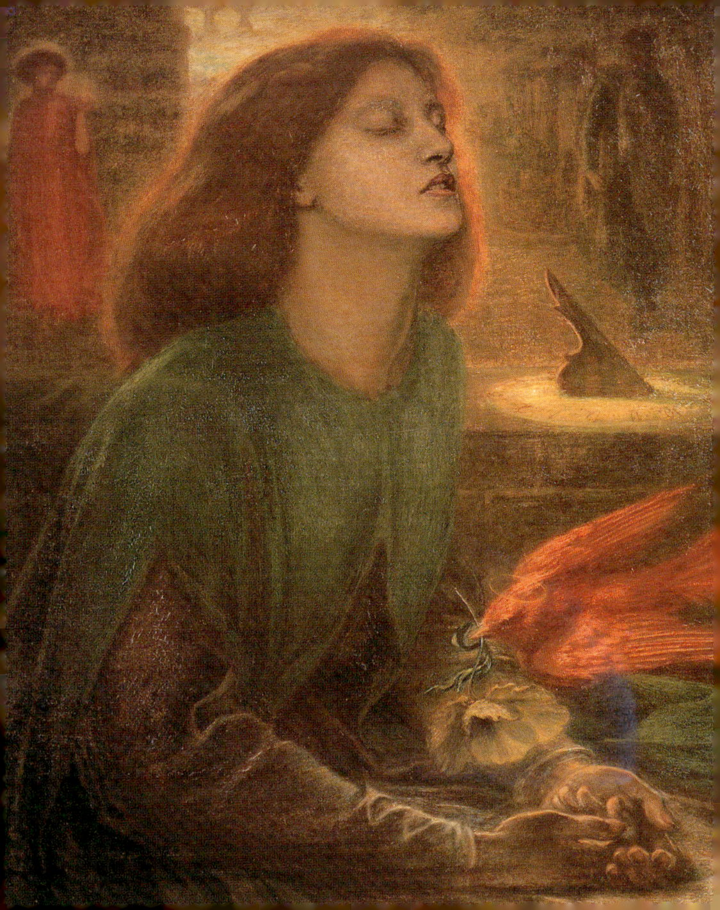

...beautie is not, as fond men misdeeme,

An outward shew of things, that onely seem.

For that same goodly hew of white and red,

With which the cheekes are sprinckled, shal decay,

And those sweete rosy leaues so fairely spred

Vpon the lips, shall fade and fall away

To that they were, euen to corrupted clay.

That golden wyre, those sparckling stars so bright

Shall turne to dust, and loose their goodly light.

But that faire lampe, from whose celestiall ray

That light proceedes, which kindleth louers fire,

Shall neuer be extinguisht nor decay.

An Hymne in Honour of Beautie
(Edmund Spenser 1552?-99)

BEATA BEATRIX
DANTE GABRIEL ROSSETTI

There is a willow grows aslant a brook,
That shows his hoar leaves in the glassy stream;
There with fantastic garlands did she come,
Of crow-flowers, nettles, daisies, and long purples,
That liberal shepherds give a grosser name,
But our cold maids do dead men's fingers call them:
There, on the pendent boughs her coronet weeds
Clambering to hang, an envious sliver broke,
When down her weedy trophies and herself
Fell in the weeping brook. Her clothes spread wide,
And, mermaid-like, awhile they bore her up...
Till that her garments, heavy with their drink,
Pull'd the poor wretch from her melodious lay
To muddy death.

Hamlet Act IV, Scene vii
(William Shakespeare 1564-1616)

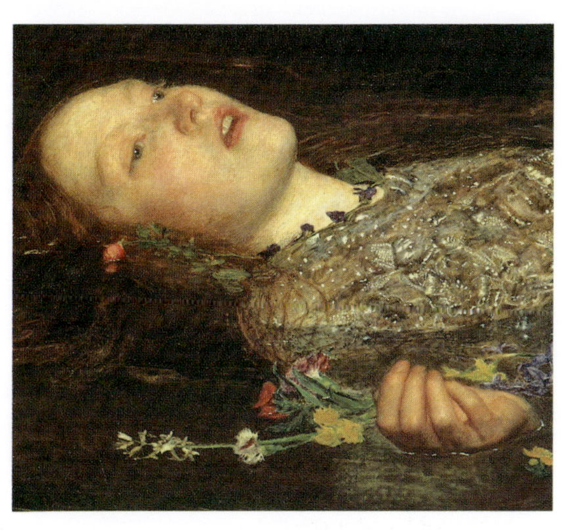

OPHELIA

JOHN EVERETT MILLAIS

DETAIL AND OVERLEAF

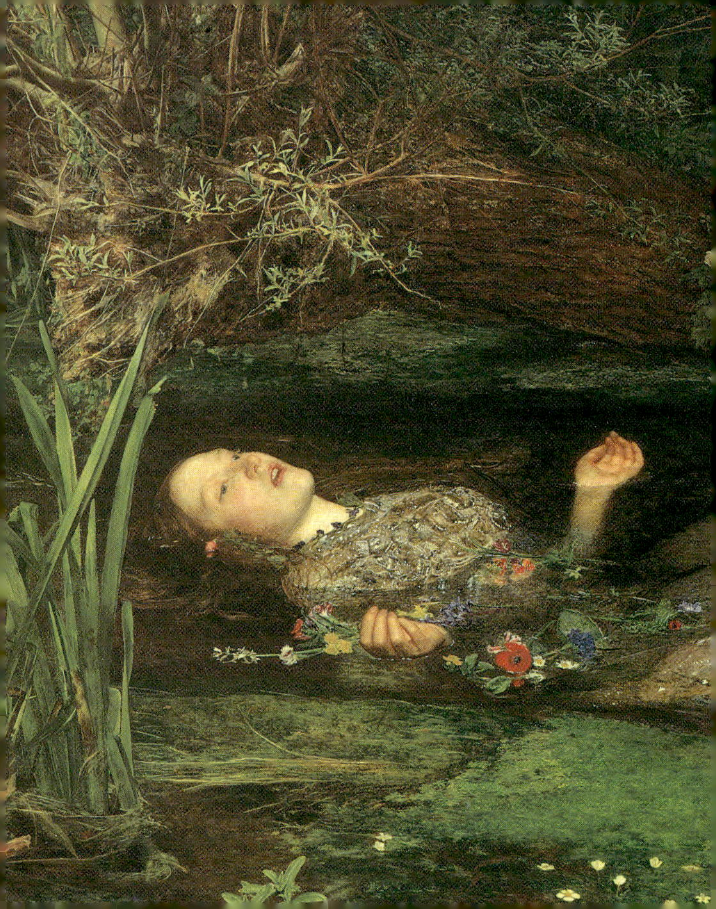

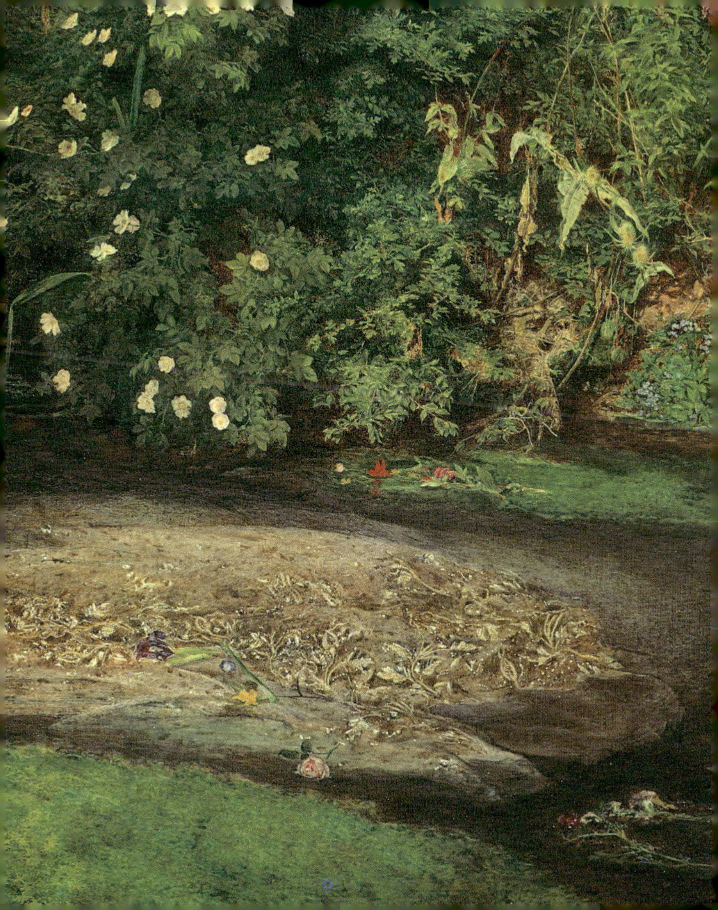

ORIANA
FREDERICK SANDYS

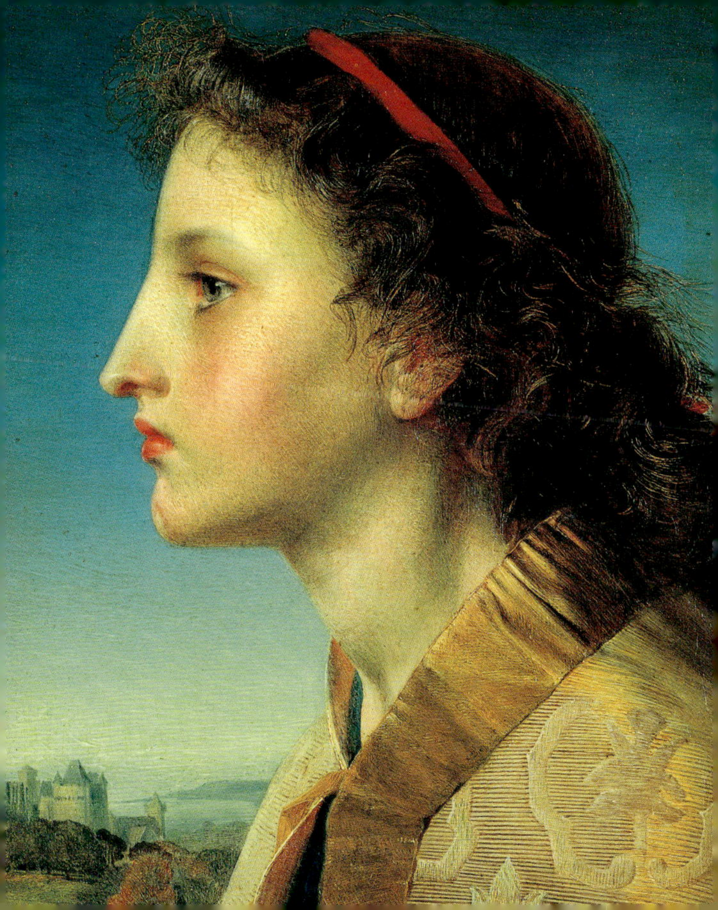

Her angel's face
As the great eye of heaven shined bright,
And made a sunshine in the shady place;
Did never mortal eye behold such heavenly grace.

The Faerie Queene
(Edmund Spenser 1552?-99)

PROSERPINE
DANTE GABRIEL ROSSETTI
DETAIL

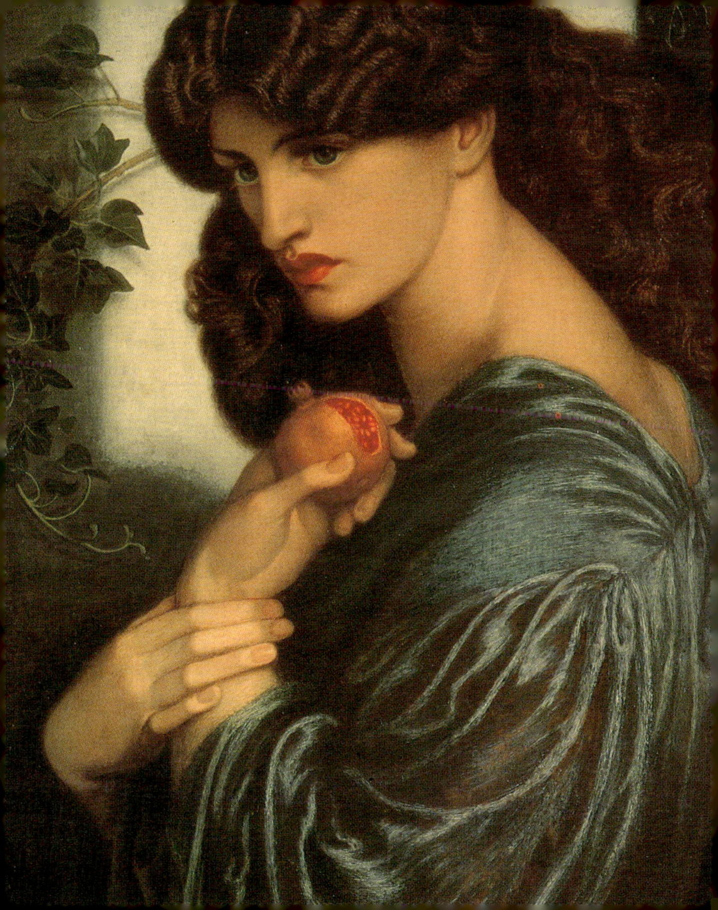

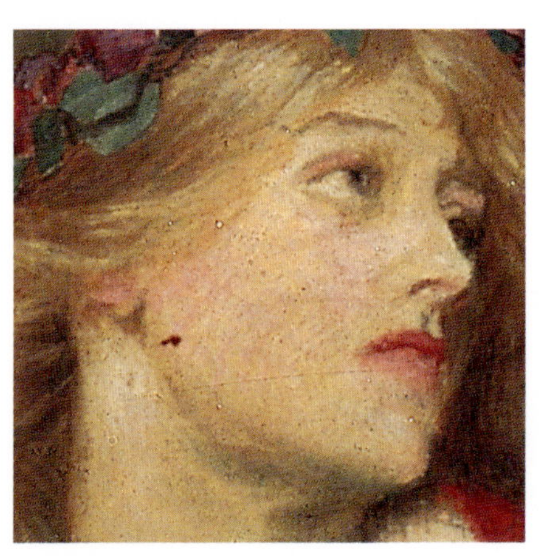

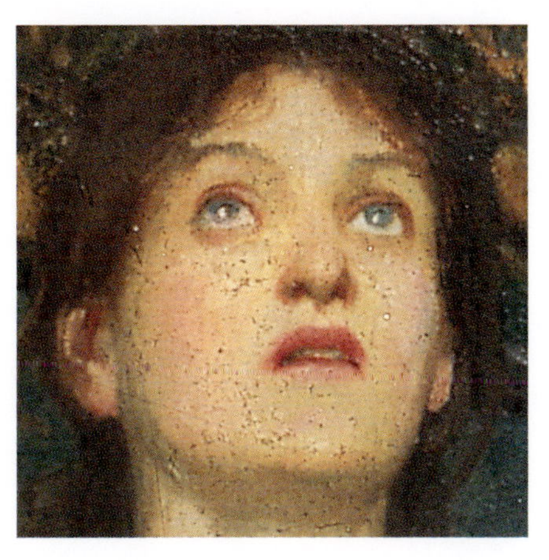

THE BLESSED DAMOZEL
JOHN BYAM SHAW
DETAILS AND OVERLEAF

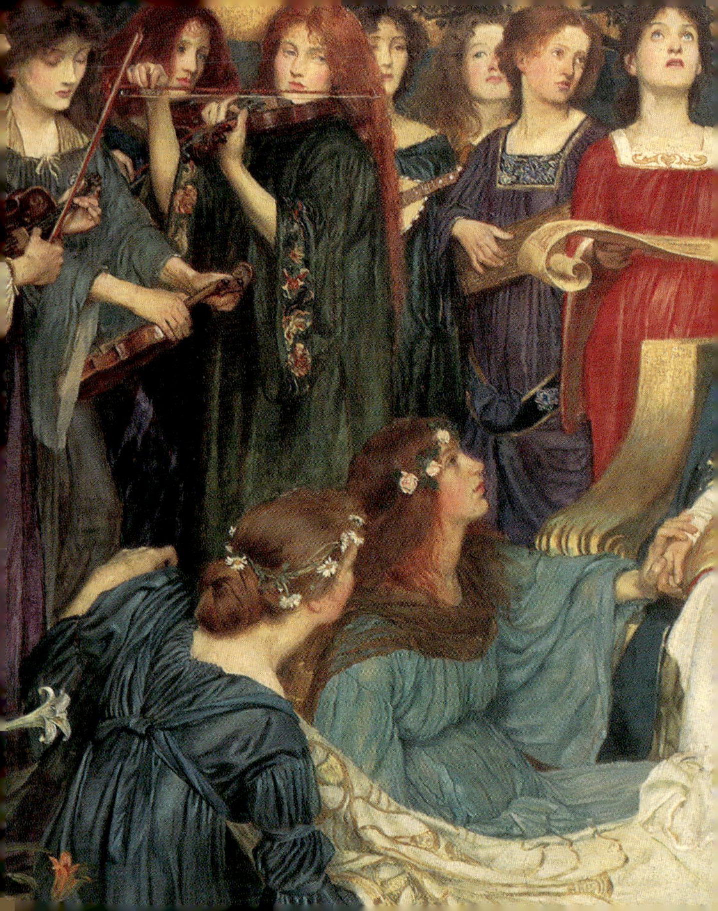

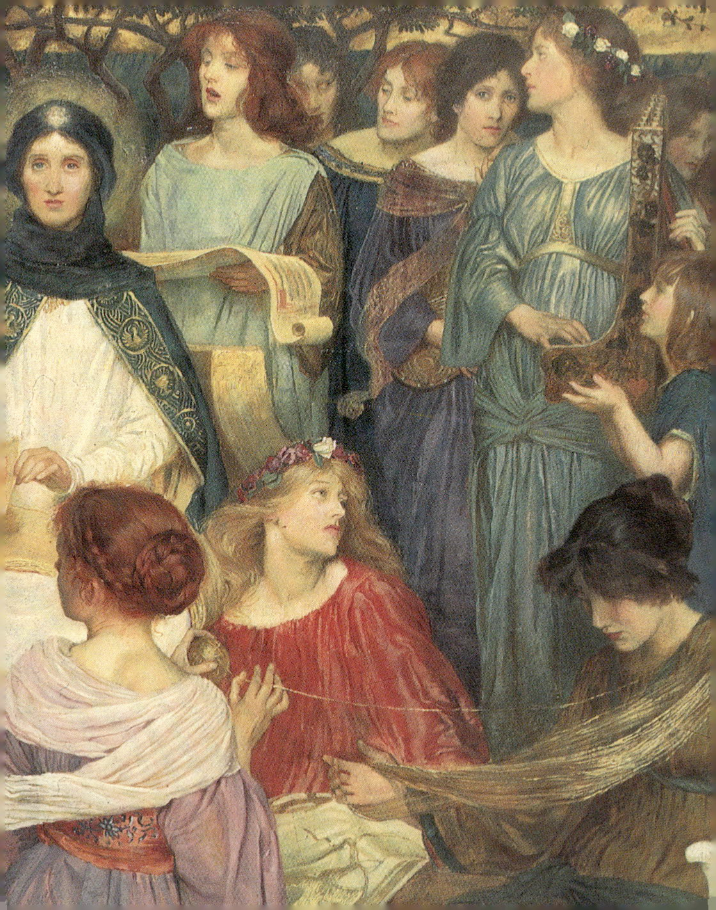

THE DAY DREAM
DANTE GABRIEL ROSSETTI

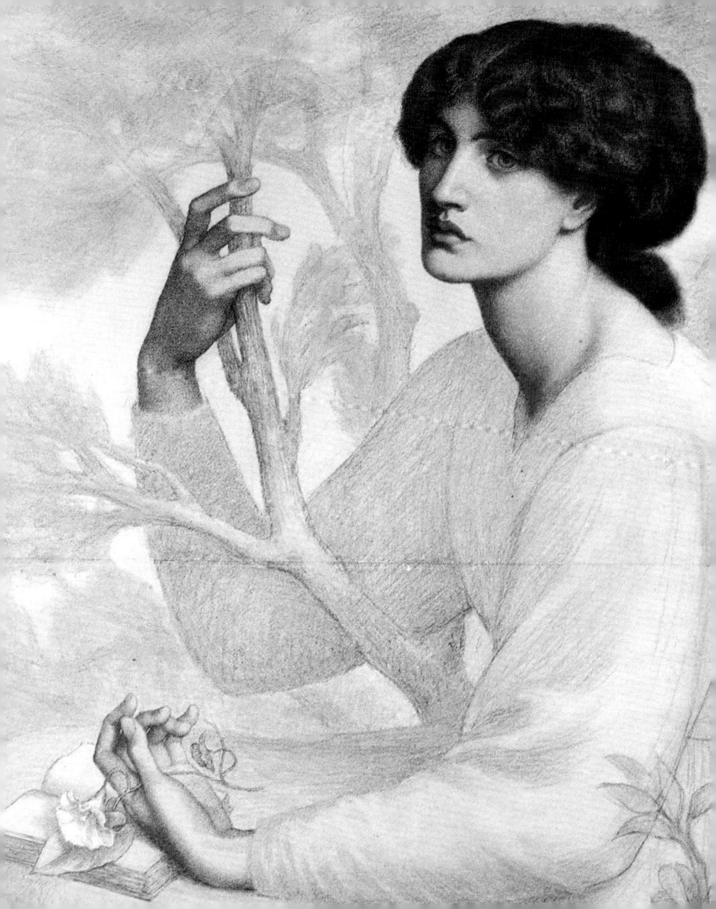

Wherever you did walk or sit
The thickest boughs could make no shade,
Although the sun had granted it;
The fairest flowers could please no more, near you,
Than painted flowers set next to them could do.

The Spring
(Abraham Cowley 1618-67)

DAY DREAM
DANTE GABRIEL ROSSETTI

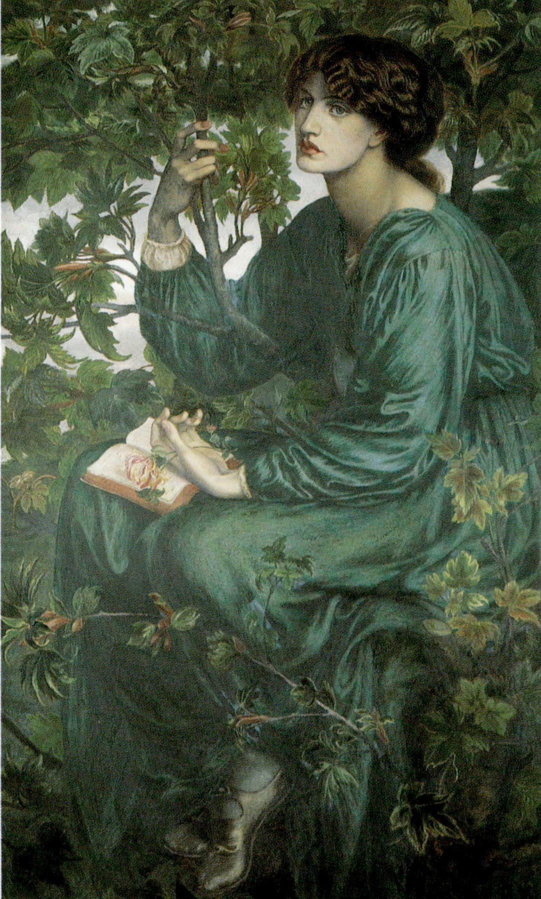

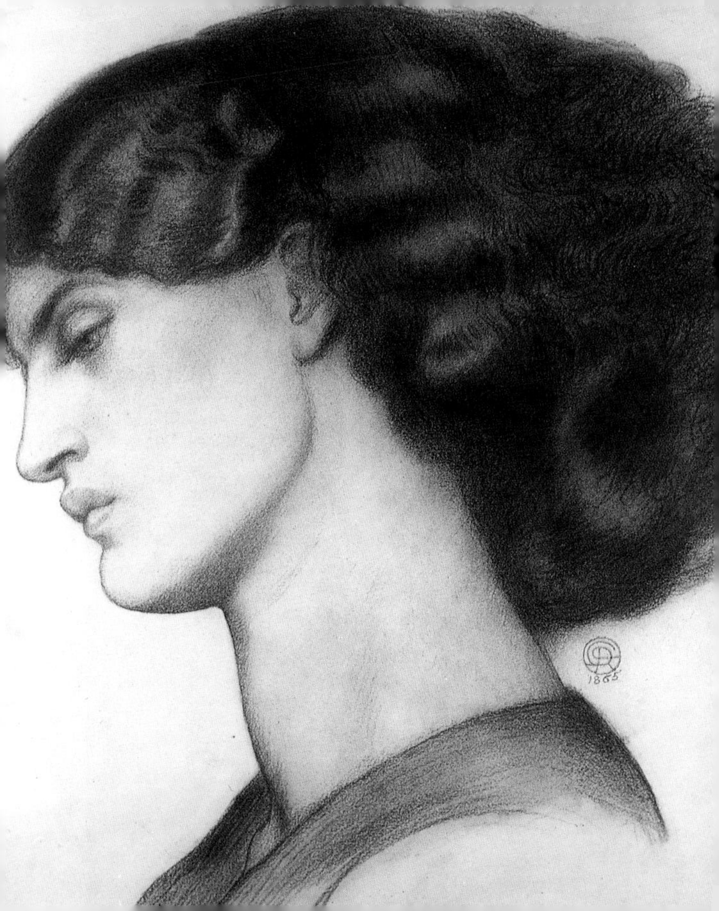

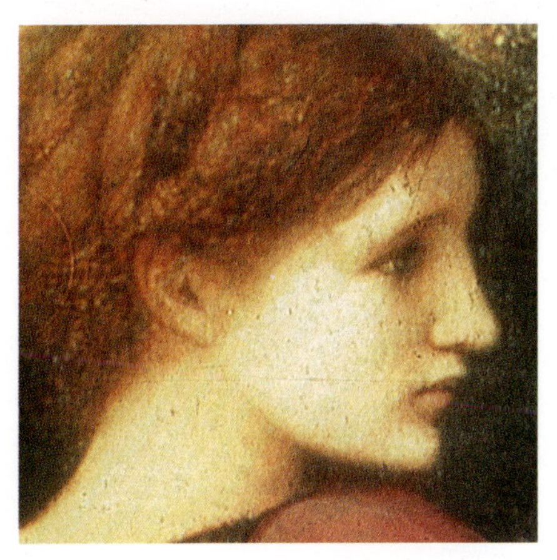

THE MILL
EDWARD BURNE-JONES
DETAIL AND OVERLEAF

―――――――

MRS WILLIAM MORRIS
DANTE GABRIEL ROSSETTI

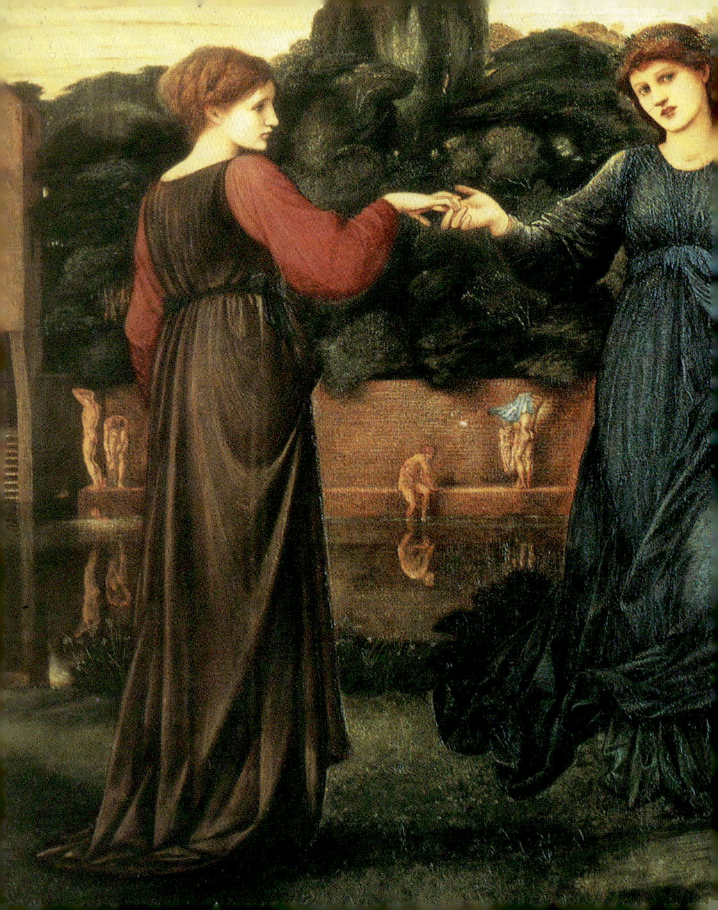

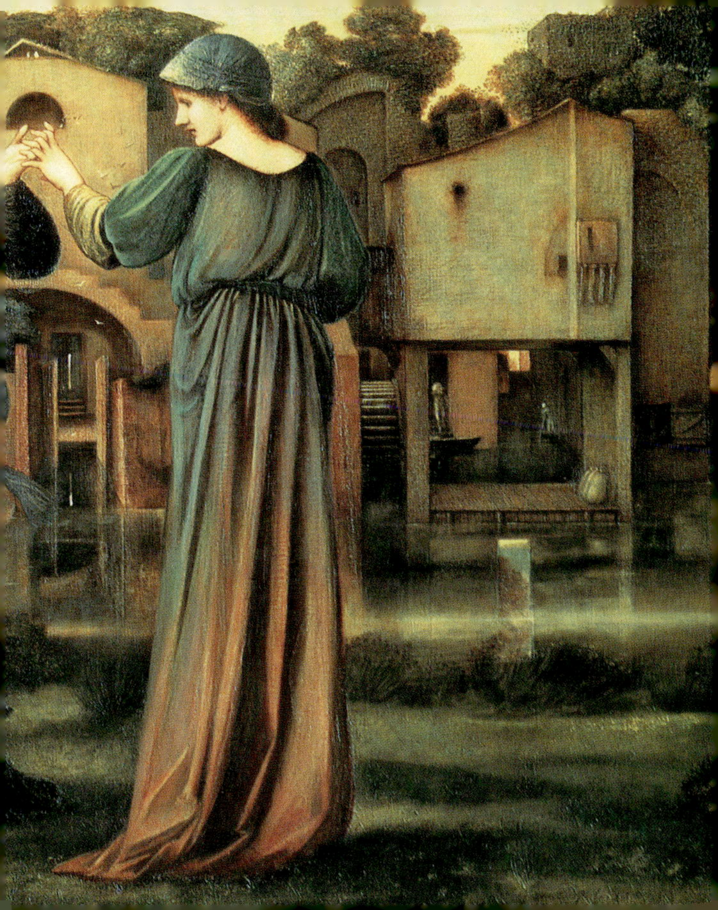

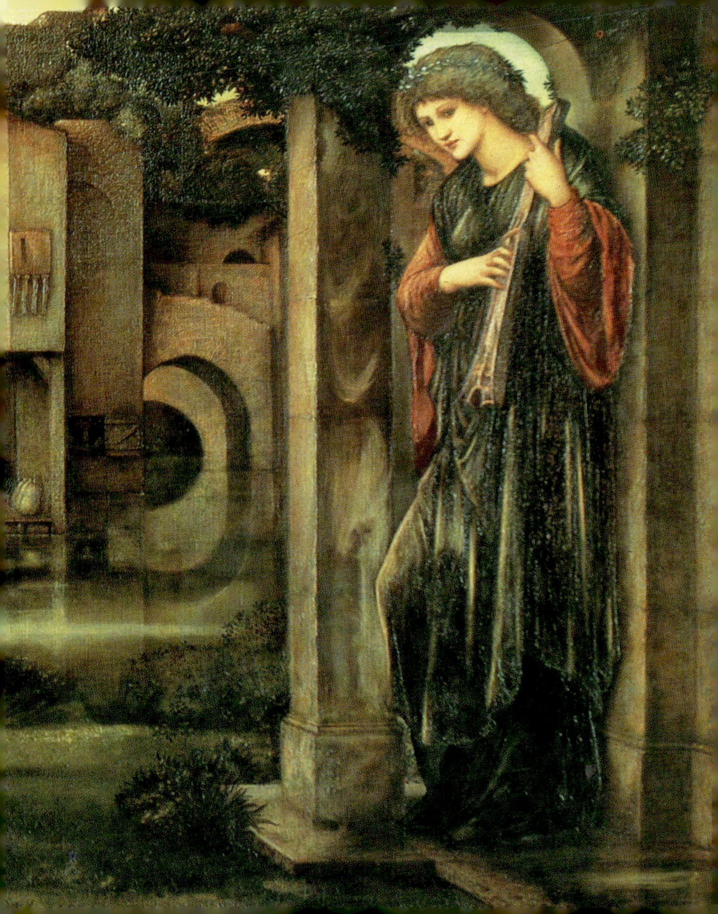

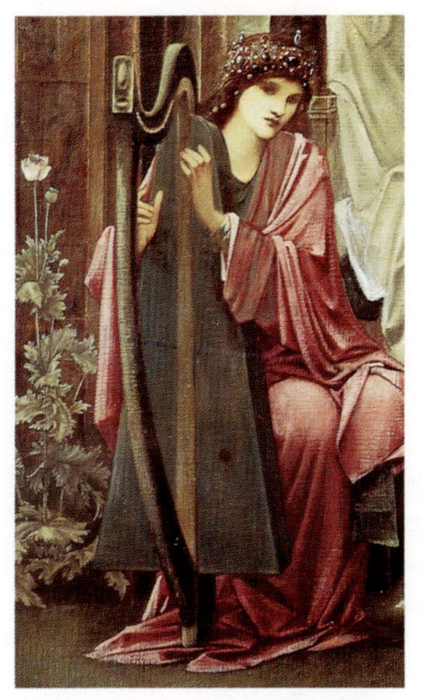

THE LAST SLEEP OF ARTHUR IN AVALON
EDWARD BURNE-JONES
DETAIL

THE MILL
EDWARD BURNE-JONES
DETAIL

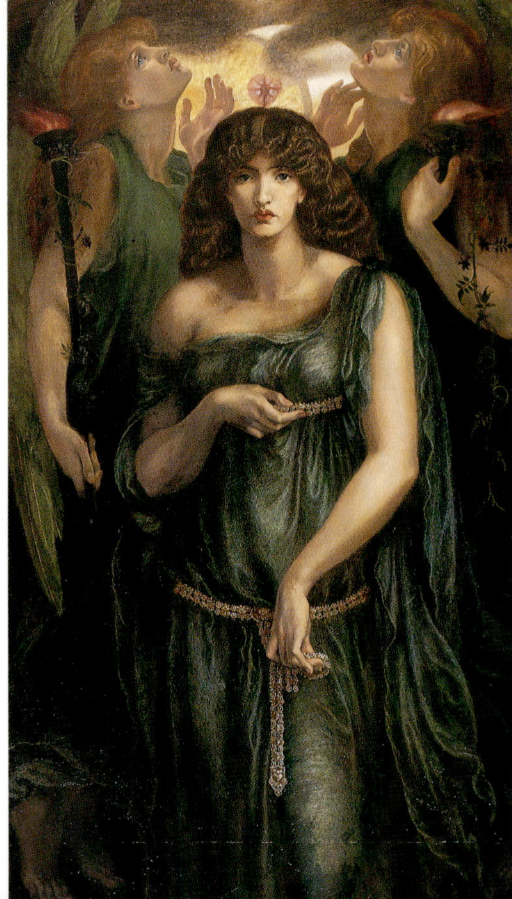

She walks in beauty, like the night
  Of cloudless climes and starry skies;
And all that's best of dark and bright
  Meet in her aspect and her eyes:

'She walks in beauty'
(Lord Byron 1788 -1824)

ASTARTE SYRIACA
DANTE GABRIEL ROSSETTI

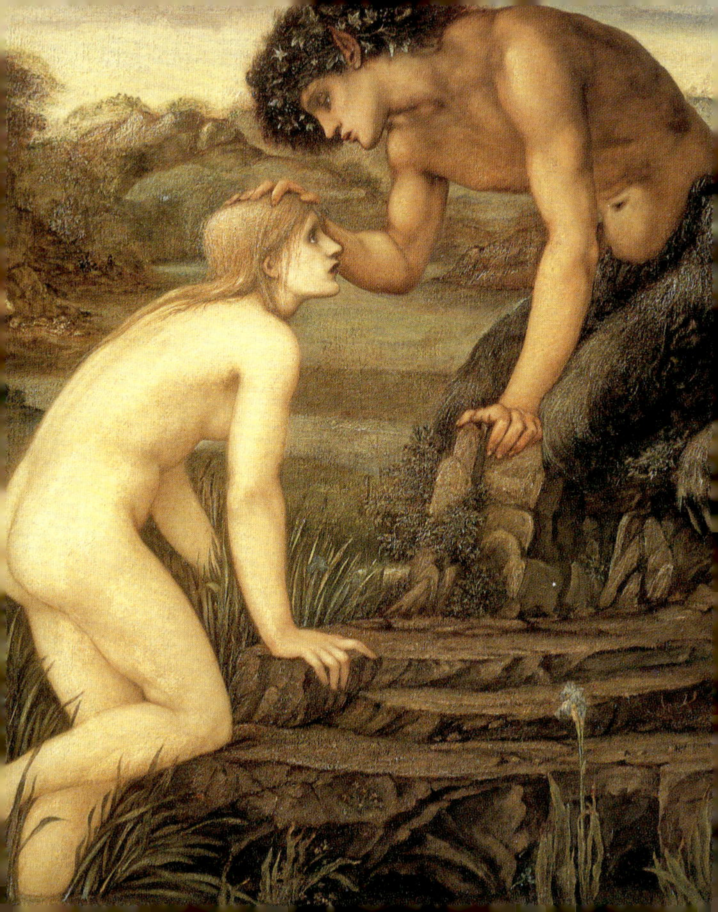

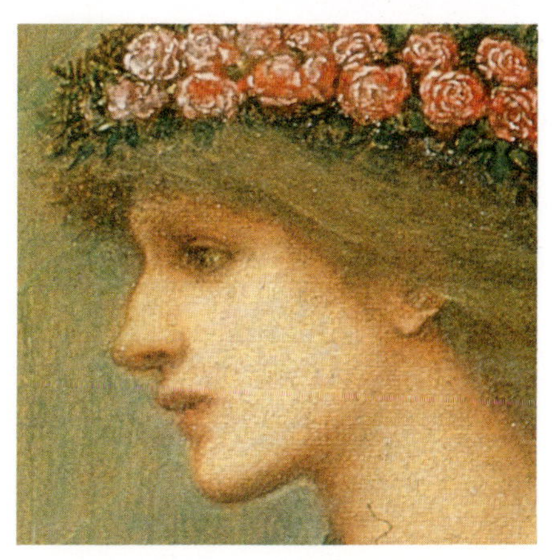

PILGRIM AT THE GATE OF IDLENESS
EDWARD BURNE-JONES
DETAIL AND OVERLEAF

———

PAN AND PSYCHE
EDWARD BURNE-JONES

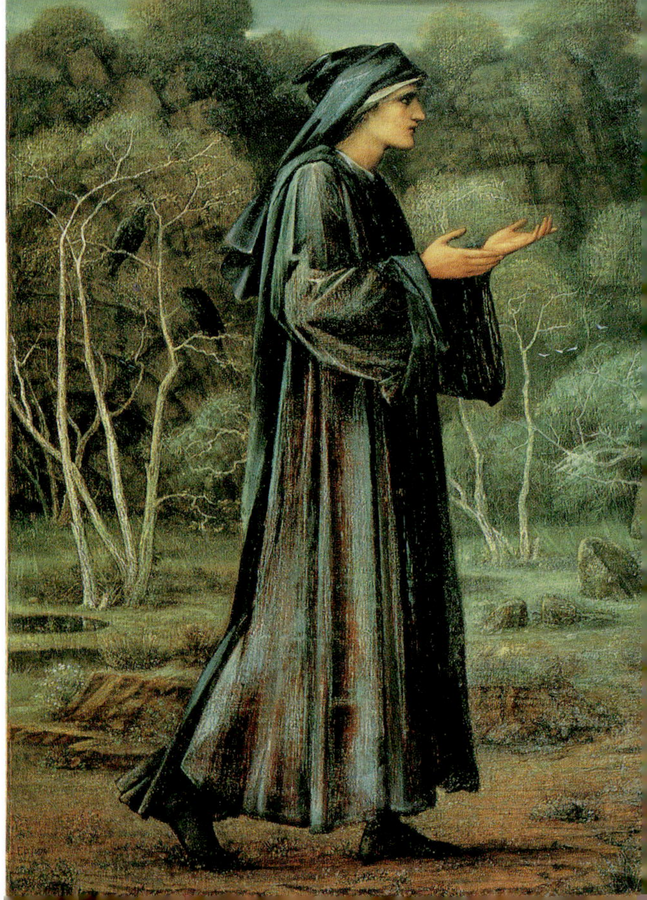

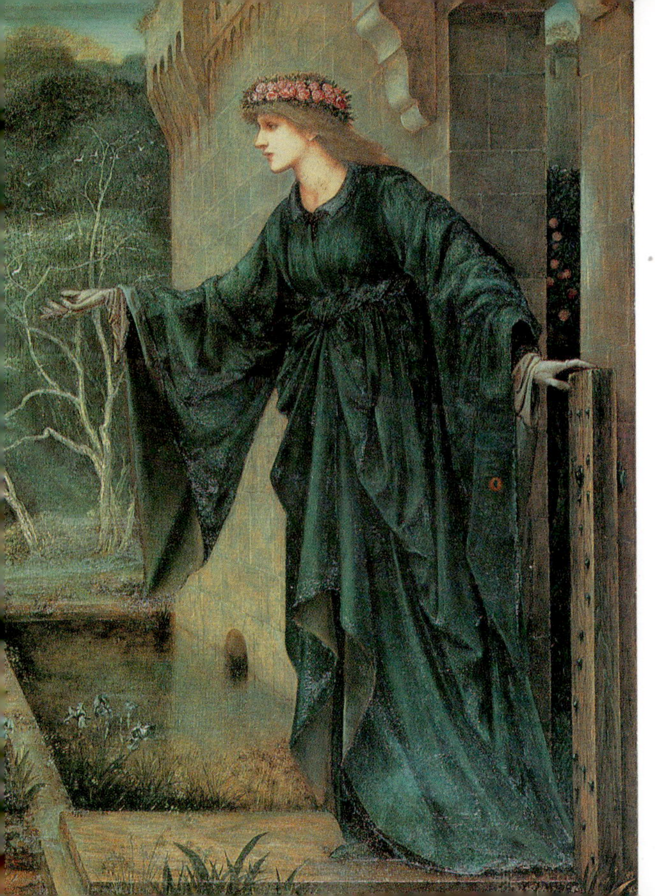

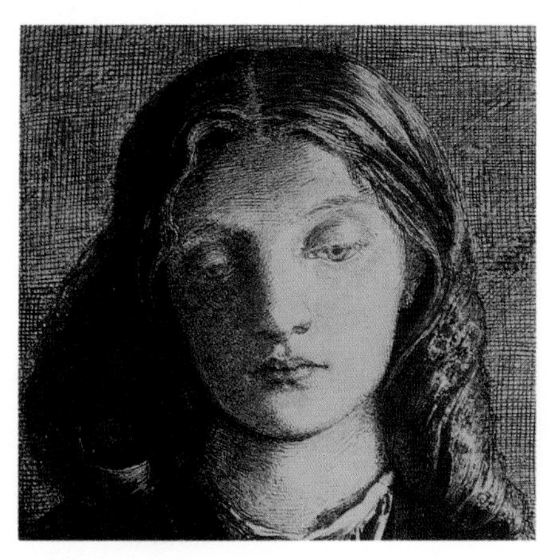

ELIZABETH SIDDAL
DANTE GABRIEL ROSSETTI

LA BARONNE MADELEINE DESLANDES
EDWARD BURNE-JONES

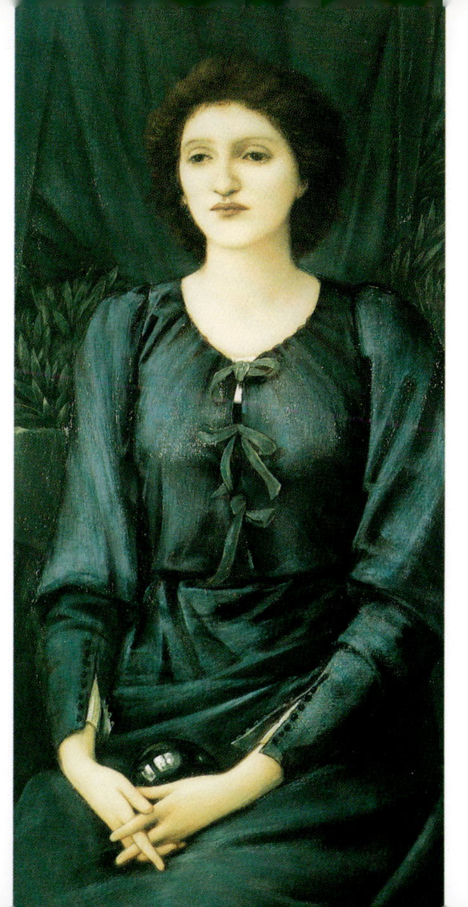

So sweet, so louely, and so mild as she,
Adornd with beautyes grace and vertues store
Her goodly eyes lyke Saphyres shining bright,
Her forehead yuory white,
Her cheekes lyke apples which the sun hath rudded,
Her lips lyke cherryes charming men to byte,

Epithalamion
(Edmund Spenser 1552?-99)

VENUS VENTICORDIA
DANTE GABRIEL ROSSETTI

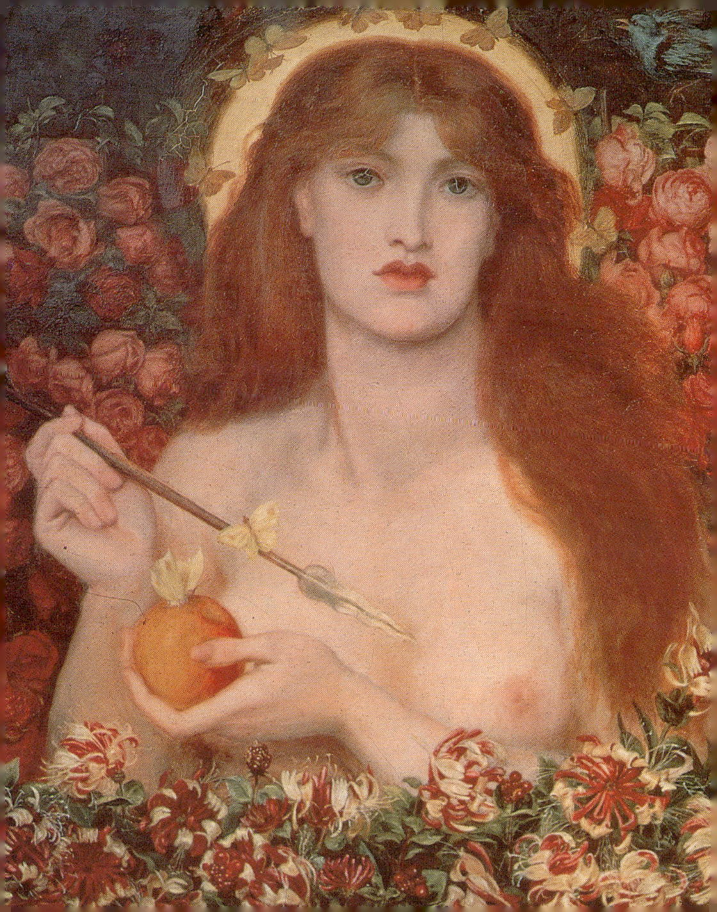

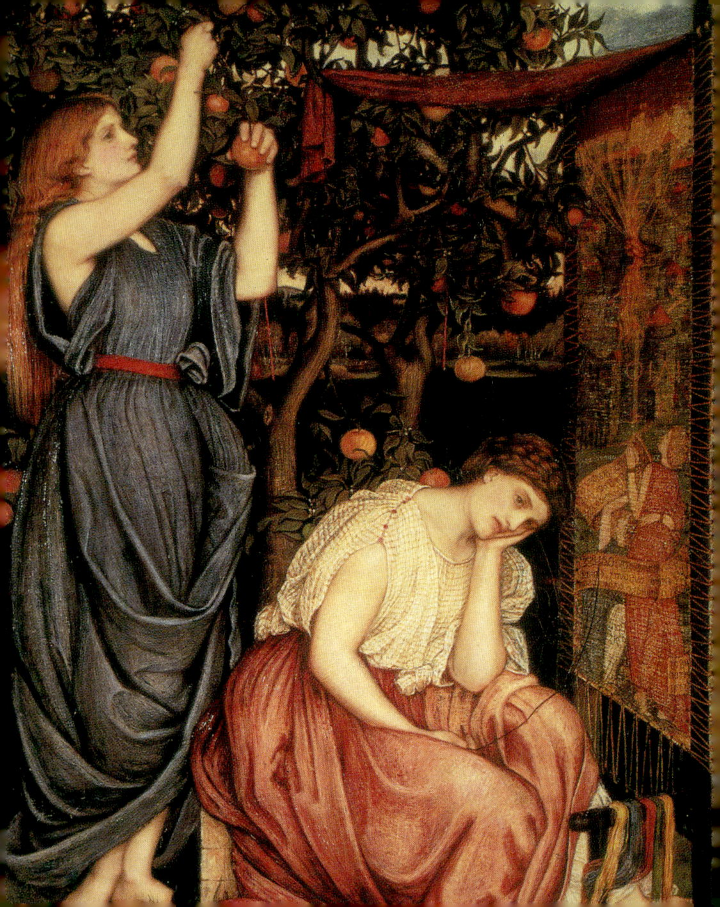

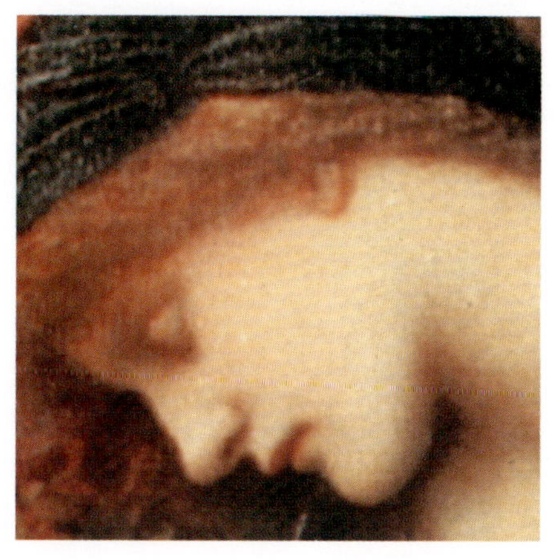

THE SLEEPING BEAUTY
EDWARD BURNE-JONES
DETAIL AND OVERLEAF

———

PENELOPE
SPENCER STANHOPE

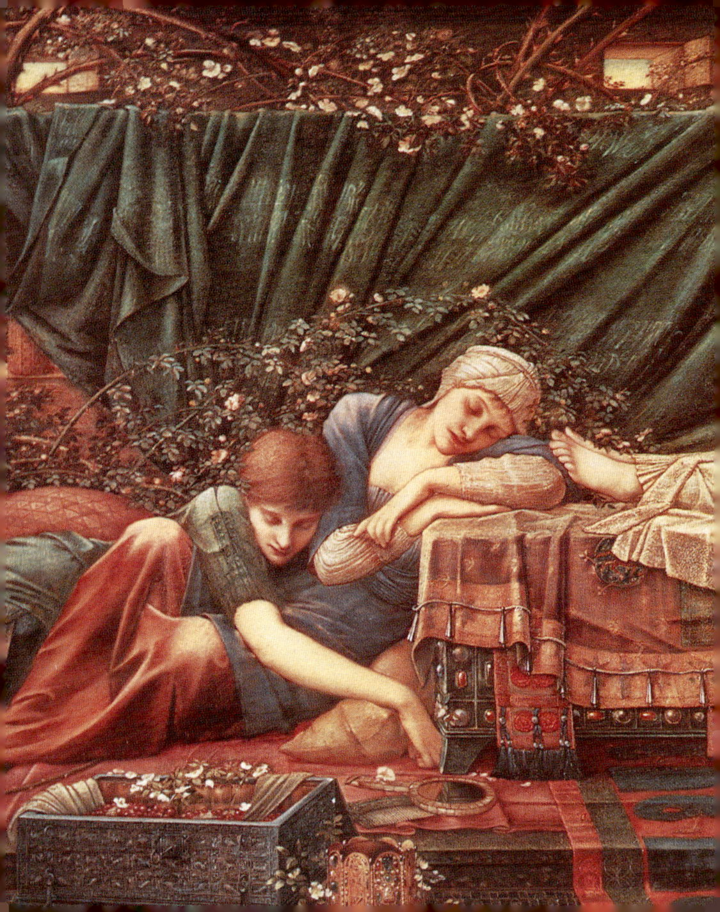

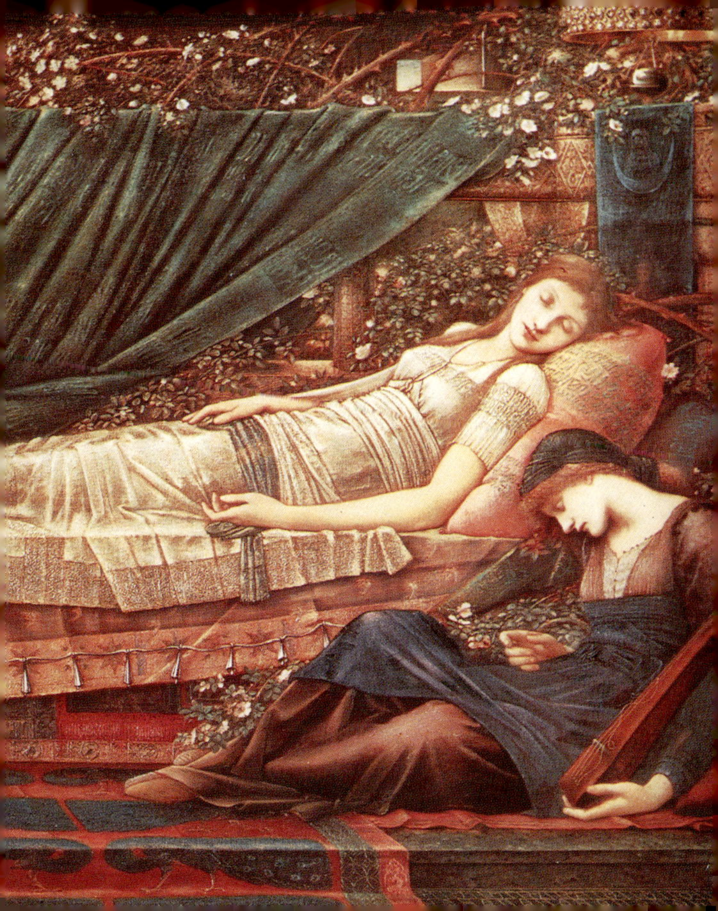

THE RED CAP

FREDERICK SANDYS

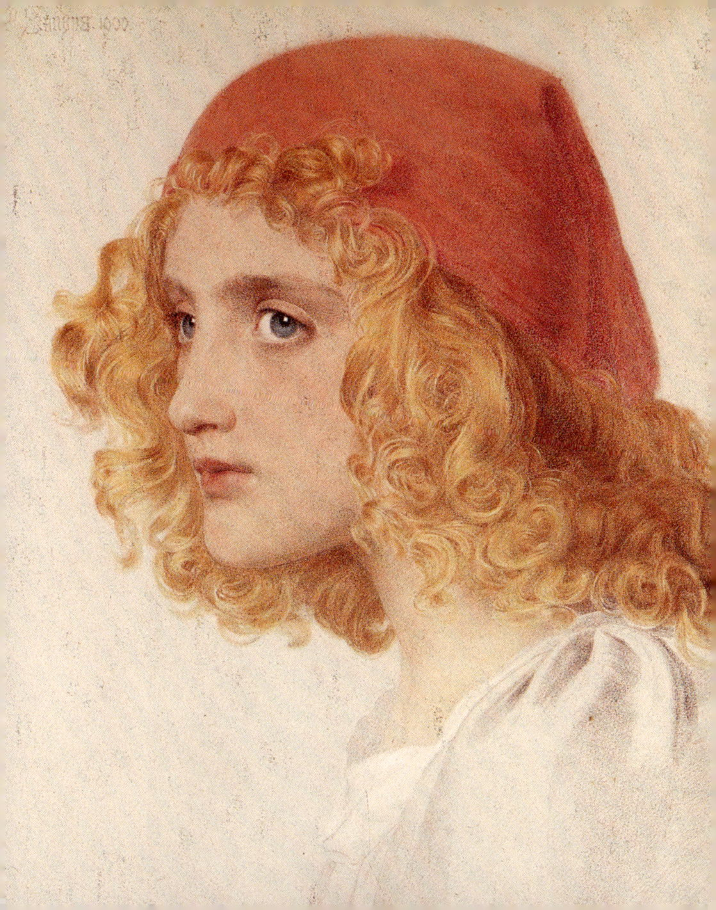

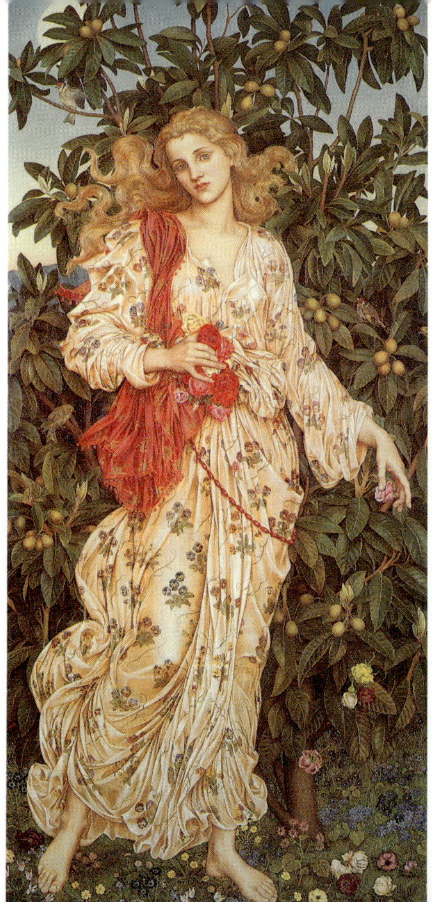

Rise and put on your foliage, and be seen
To come forth, like the spring-time, fresh and green,
    And sweet as Flora. Take no care
    For jewels for your gown or hair:
    Fear not; the leaves will strew
    Gems in abundance upon you:

Corinna's Going a-Maying
(Robert Herrick 1591-1674)

FLORA
EVELYN DE MORGAN

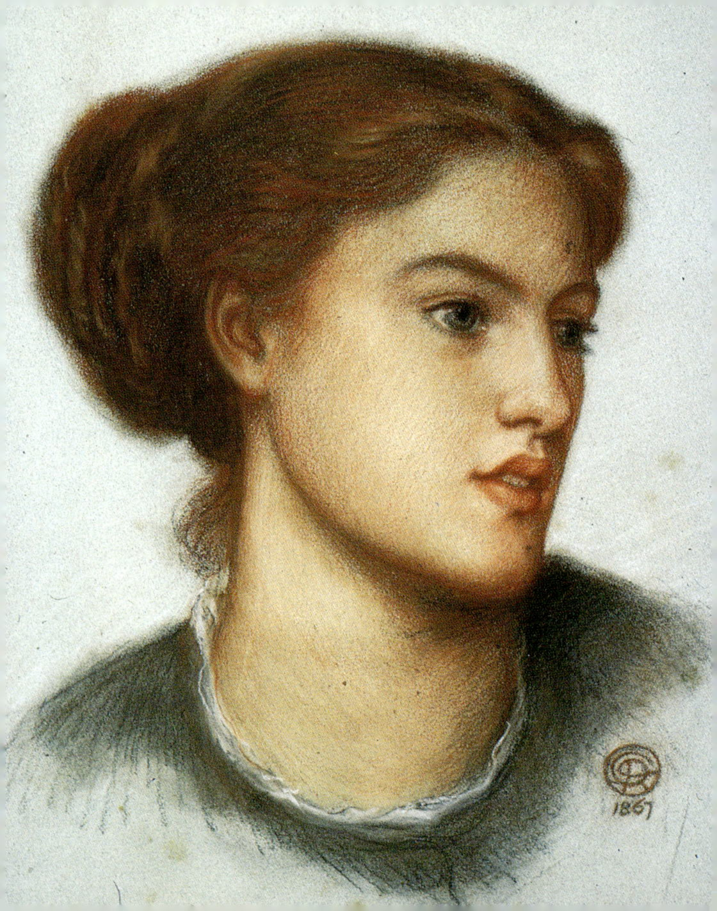

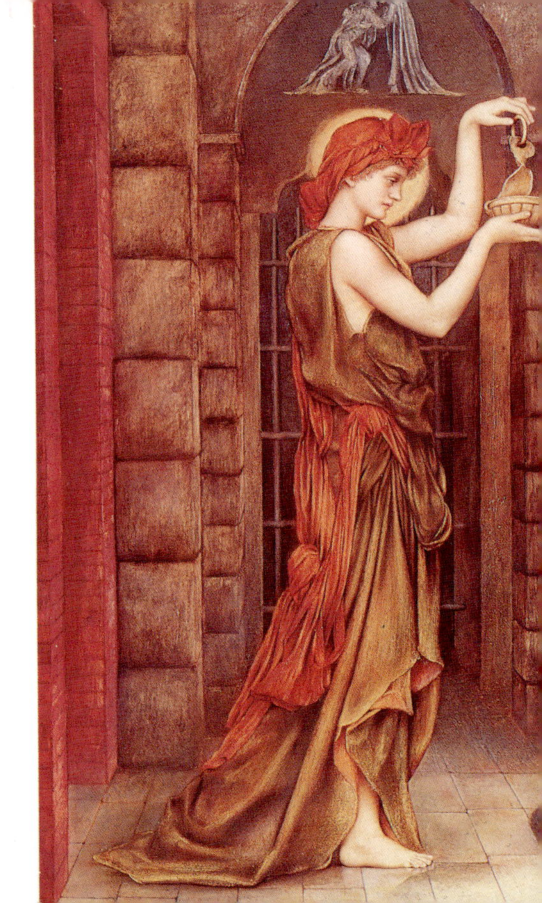

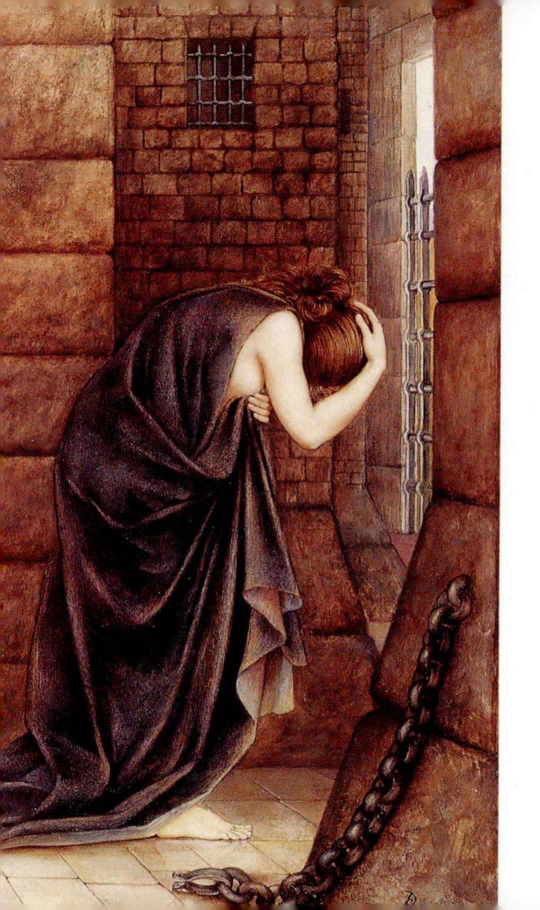

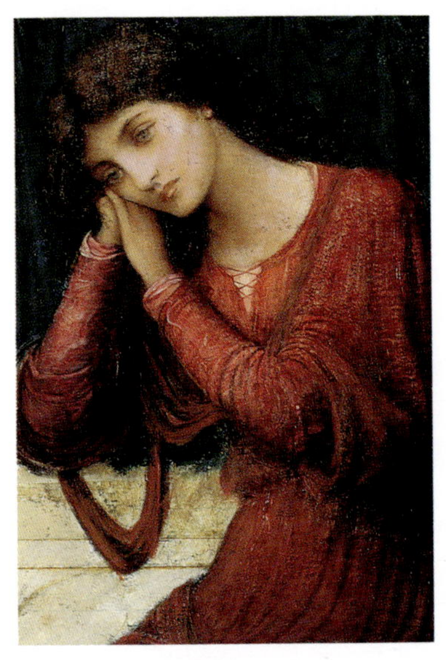

WHEN SORROW COMES IN SUMMER DAYS,
ROSES BLOOM IN VAIN
JOHN MELHUISH STRUDWICK

———

MRS BEYER
DANTE GABRIEL ROSSETTI

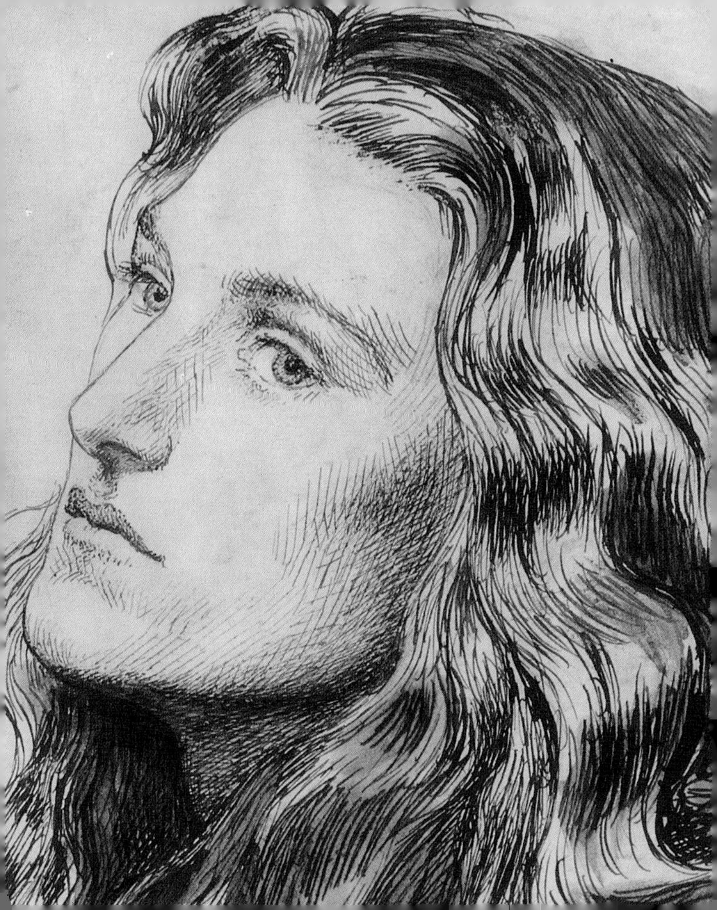

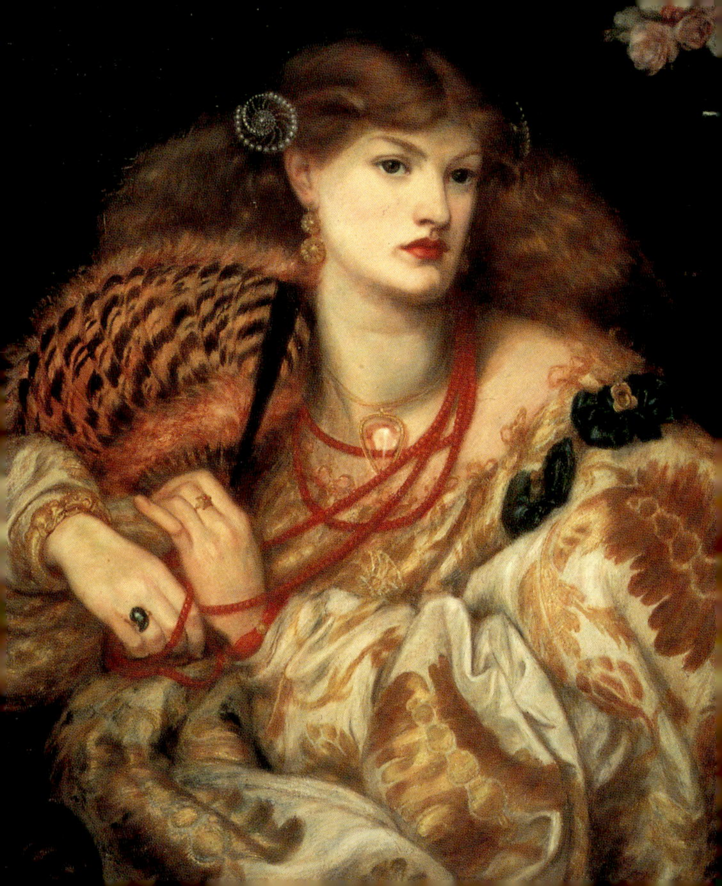

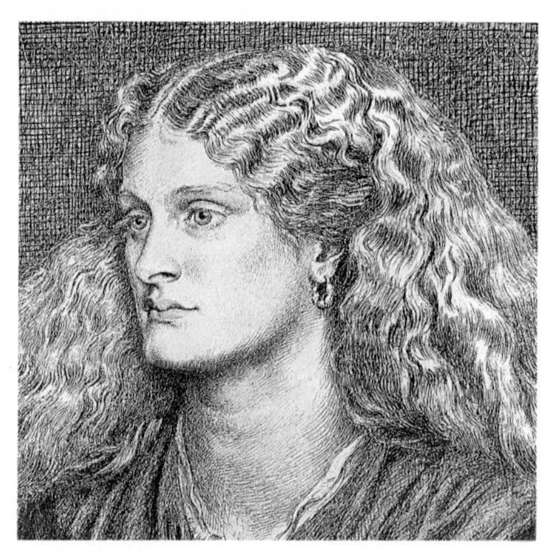

ANNIE MILLER
DANTE GABRIEL ROSSETTI

———

MONNA VANNA
DANTE GABRIEL ROSSETTI

My mistress' eyes are nothing like the sun;
Coral is far more red than her lips' red.
If snow be white, why then her breasts are dun;
If hairs be wires, black wires grow on her head.
I have seen roses damask'd, red and white,
But no such roses see I in her cheeks;
And in some perfumes is there more delight
Than in the breath that from my mistress reeks.
I love to hear her speak, yet well I know
That music hath a far more pleasing sound.
I grant I never saw a goddess go:
My mistress when she walks treads on the ground.
   And yet, by heaven, I think my love as rare
   As any she belied with false compare.

Sonnets CXXX
(William Shakespeare 1564-1616)

THE LADY OF PITY
DANTE GABRIEL ROSSETTI

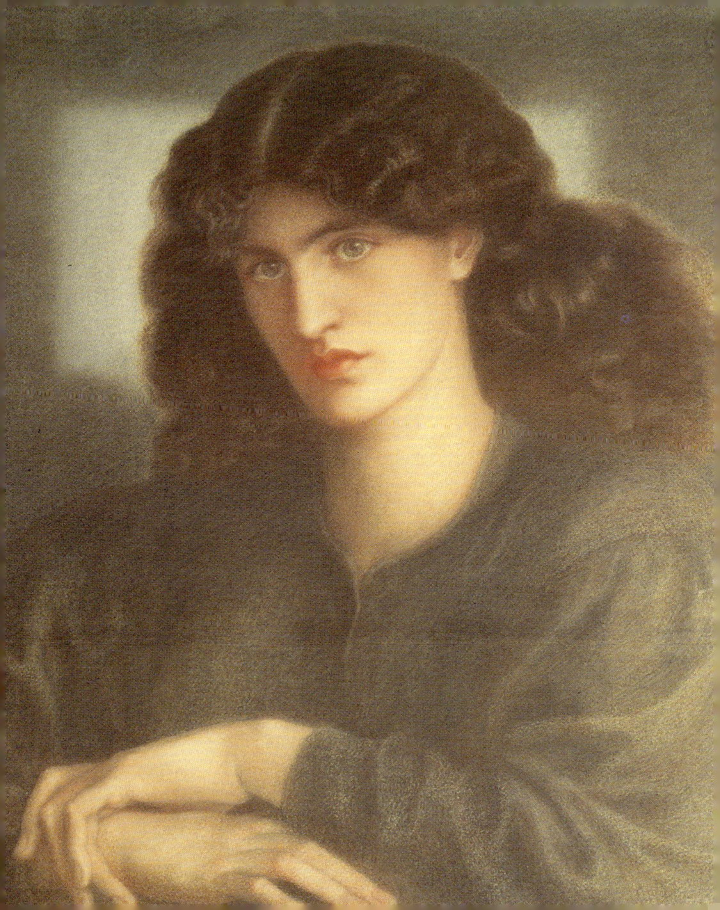

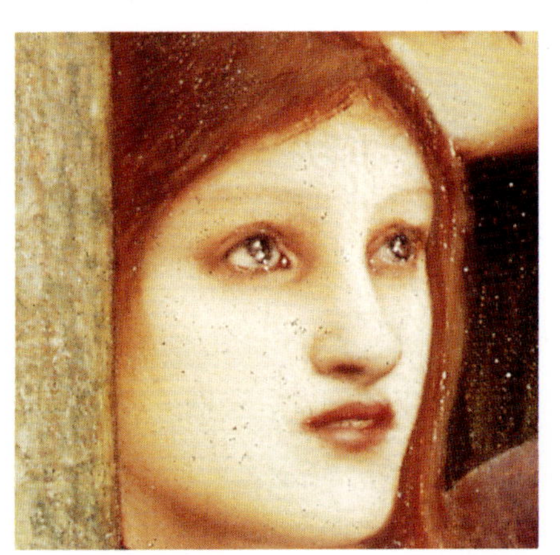

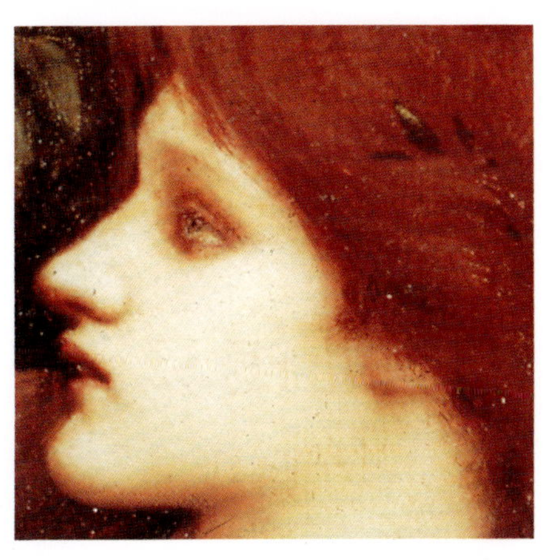

THE BALEFUL HEAD
EDWARD BURNE-JONES
DETAILS AND OVERLEAF

THE BALEFUL HEAD
EDWARD BURNE-JONES

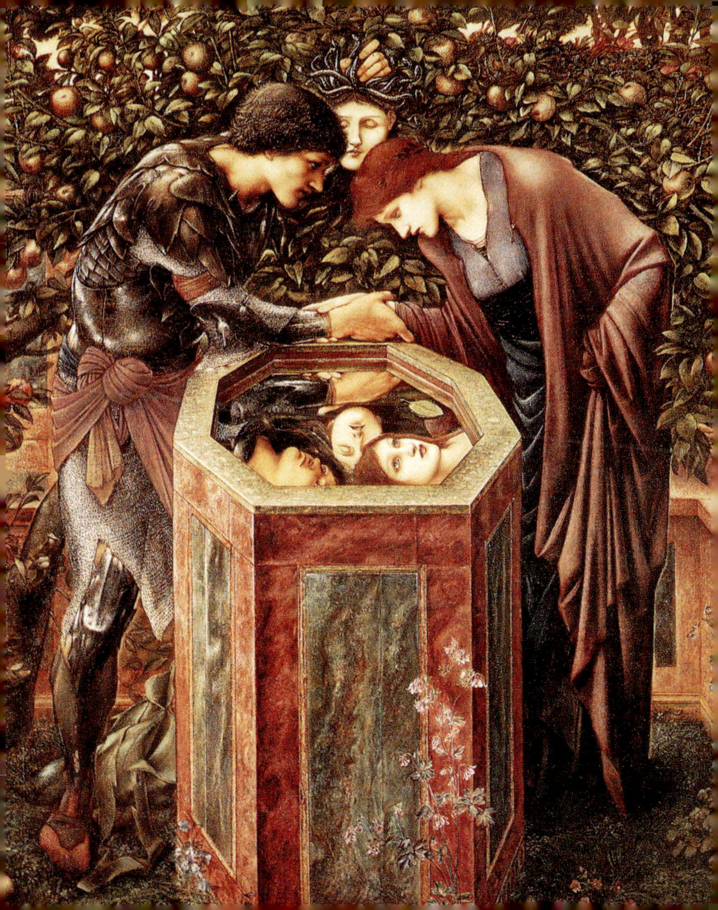

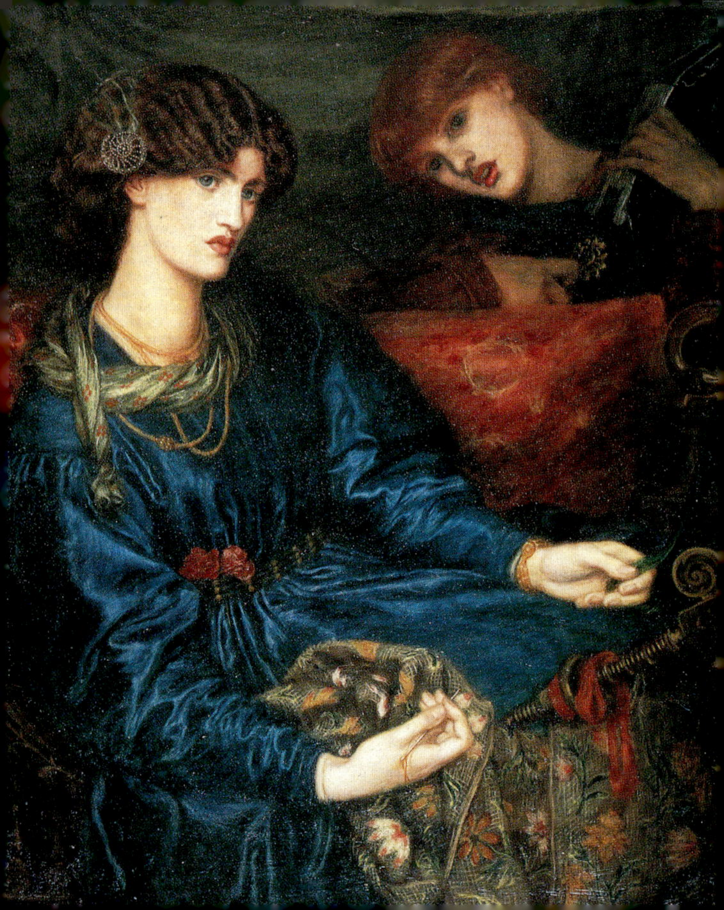

Take, O take those lips away,
That so sweetly were forsworn;
And those eyes, the break of day,
Lights that do mislead the morn:
But my kisses bring again,
          Bring again;
Seals of love, but seal'd in vain,
          Seal'd in vain.

Measure for Measure Act IV, Scene i
(William Shakespeare 1564-1616)

MARIANA
DANTE GABRIEL ROSSETTI

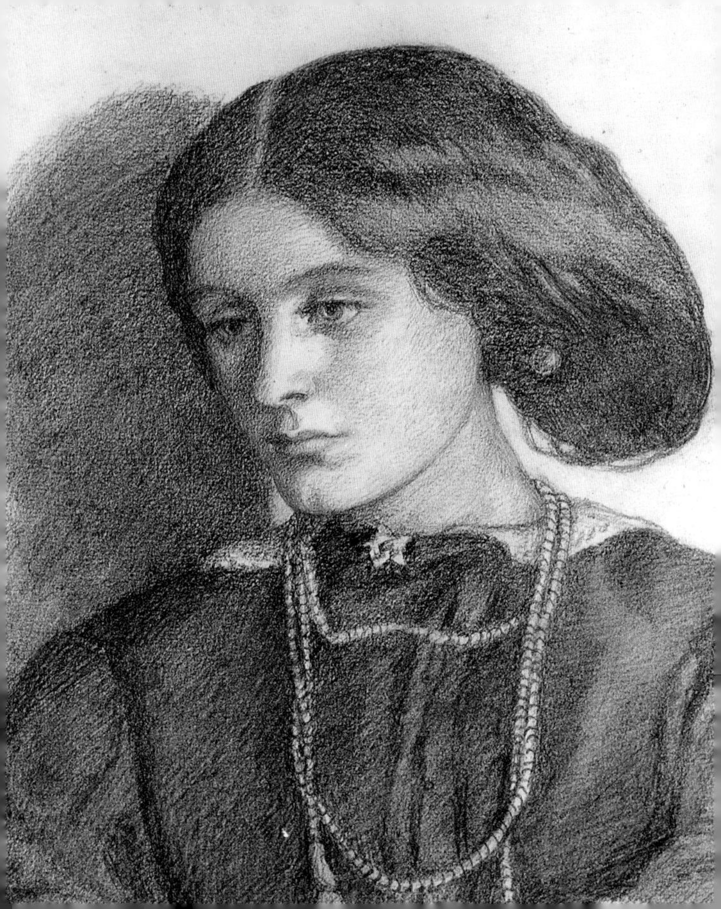

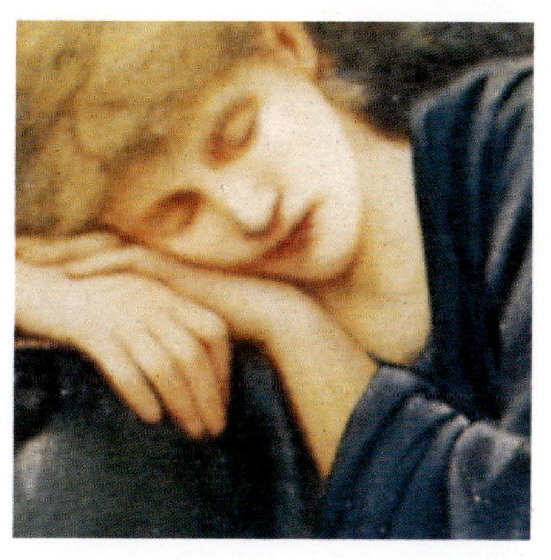

THE GARDEN COURT
EDWARD BURNE-JONES
DETAIL AND OVERLEAF

MRS BURNE-JONES
DANTE GABRIEL ROSSETTI

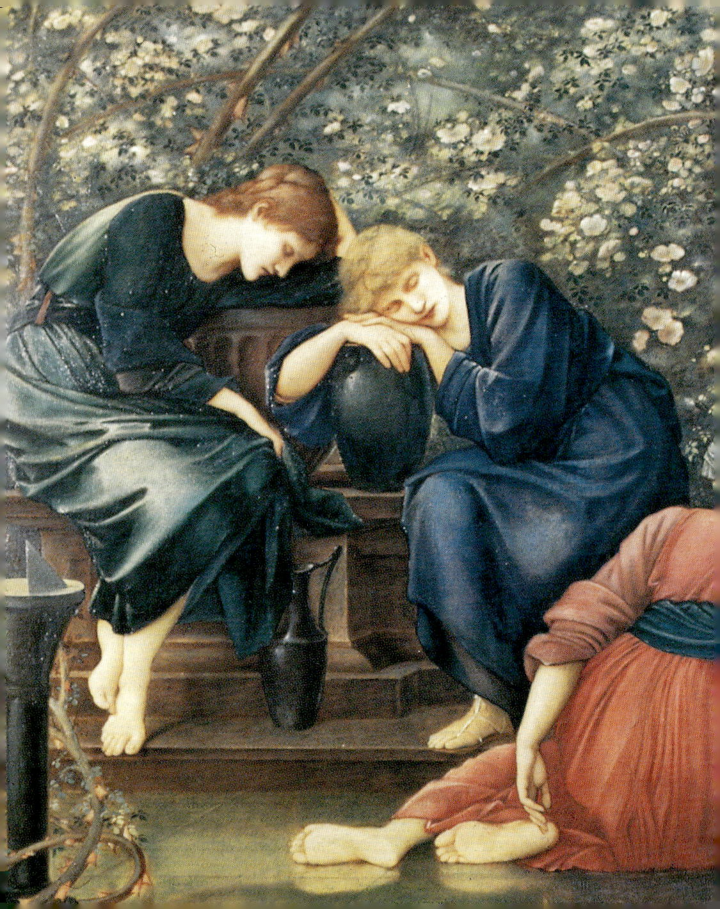

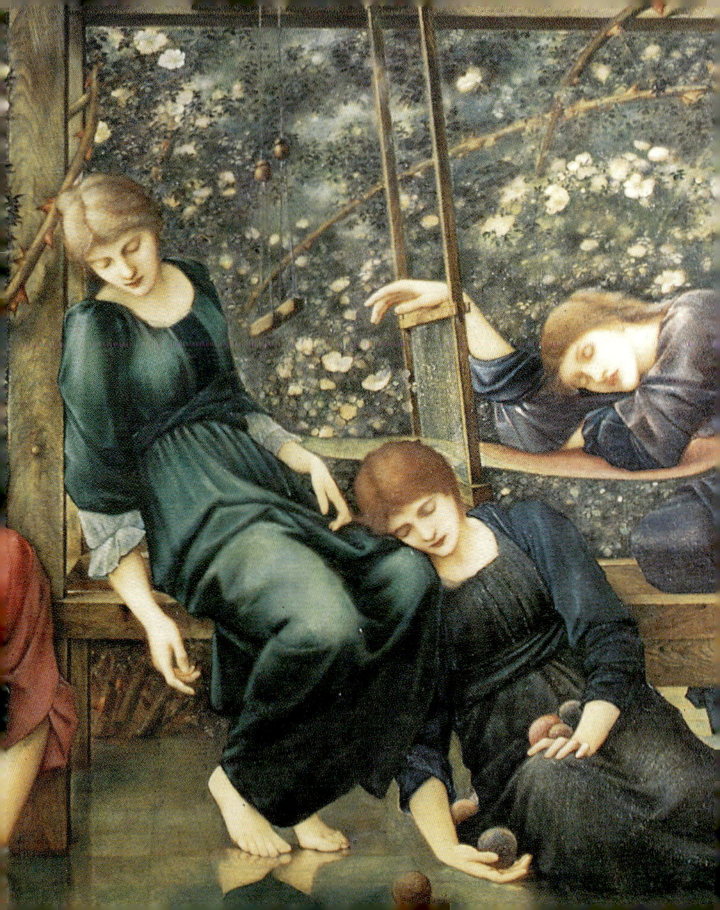

EDWARD BURNE-JONES (1833-98)

Born in the West Midlands but of Welsh descent, Burne-Jones was the son of a Birmingham frame-maker. His early vocation for the priesthood was diverted during his studies at Exeter College, Oxford, when he met William Morris and developed a keen interest in art. He first saw the work of Dante Gabriel Rossetti and other members of the Pre-Raphaelite Brotherhood in a private collection owned by the director of the Clarendon Press and he contrived to meet Rossetti shortly afterwards in London. Acting on his advice, Burne-Jones abandoned his scholarly life at the university to pursue an artistic career and joined Rossetti's team of artists in decorating the Oxford Union.

In 1859, Burne-Jones travelled to Italy to study the work of Botticelli and returned there several years later with John Ruskin, journeying to Venice to copy paintings by Tintoretto. Burne-Jones's tempestuous affair with Marie Zambaco, who posed for him nude, sparked the controversy that raged over the indecency of his painting *Phyllis and Demophoön*, finally exploding in his resignation from the Old Watercolour Society in 1870. The opening of the Grosvenor Gallery in 1877 with a major collection of his work established Burne-Jones as a public figure. Following his success at the Paris Exhibition in 1878 he was honoured by an invitation from the French government to represent Great Britain at the International Exhibition of Contemporary Art, together with Lord Leighton. He died in London only four years after being made a baronet by Queen Victoria.

ARTHUR HUGHES (1830-1915)

A painter and book illustrator, Hughes studied and
exhibited at the Royal Academy. In 1850, he read a
copy of *The Germ*, the short-lived journal of the Pre-
Raphaelites, and was converted to their philosophy.
He collaborated on painting the Oxford Union
murals, a venture initiated by Rossetti. Although not
acknowledged as a major painter he is noted for his
poetic sensitivity and exquisite draughtsmanship. The
1850s witnessed his most productive years, composing
The Long Engagement, possibly his most famous work,
in 1859. He also worked with Rossetti's sister, Christina
Rossetti, in illustrating her book of children's verse,
Sing Song, in 1872. Hughes' later years were spent in
suburban obscurity, although he was awarded a Civil
List pension in 1912. He died a recluse.

WILLIAM HOLMAN HUNT (1827-1910)

The eldest son of a warehouse manager, Hunt worked
as an estate agent's clerk, taking art lessons in his spare
time. As a member of the Royal Academy Schools
from 1843, Hunt formed an intense friendship with
John Everett Millais and Dante Gabriel Rossetti with
whom he founded the Pre-Raphaelite Brotherhood.
Hunt's earnest approach, moral fortitude and
painstaking attention to detail made him a key figure
in the movement. He travelled to the continent in
1849 to discover the roots of his style in the work of the
Flemish primitives. In 1854 he made the first of several
pilgrimages to biblical sites in Egypt and the Holy
Land in order to paint the realistic local landscapes
that appear in *The Scapegoat* and *The Light of the World*.
Although for years he was infatuated by his model

Annie Miller, by 1859 his passion had faded and he married Fanny Waugh in 1866. Shortly after his marriage his wife died and, since it was illegal in Great Britain, in 1875 he eloped to France to wed her sister, Edith. In 1905 he published *Pre-Raphaelitism and the Pre-Raphaelite Brotherhood*, an autobiographical survey of the movement, and was awarded the Order of Merit in the same year. He is buried in St Paul's Cathedral in London.

JOHN EVERETT MILLAIS (1829-96)

At the age of eleven Millais became the youngest student ever to be admitted to the Royal Academy Schools. Early in his career scandal erupted over *The Carpenter's Shop*, which offended Victorian propriety and provoked the fury of Charles Dickens because of its realistic depiction of the Holy Family. Bitter accusations of blasphemy and rumoured connections with the Anglo-Catholic movement were deflected by Ruskin, one of his strongest champions. This alliance with Ruskin was broken when Millais married Ruskin's former wife, Effie Gray, in 1854. Ruskin was aggrieved even though his marriage to Effie had been unconsummated and consequently annulled. Although his technical gifts made Millais a leading member of the Pre-Raphaelite Brotherhood, he savoured public acclaim and employed his talents in creating more popular images. Painting fashionable works such as *Bubbles*, commissioned by Pears & Co. to advertise their soap, and illustrating books, such as Anthony Trollope's novels and Alfred, Lord Tennyson's poems, earned him the accolade of being the most highly-paid artist of his age. Later in his career he worked on portraiture which also proved to be financially

rewarding and merited a baronetcy. He died in 1896
from cancer of the throat, an illness which had plagued
his last years forcing him to resign from the Presidency
of the Royal Academy.

ALBERT JOSEPH MOORE (1830-94)

Born in York, Moore was the fourteenth child of a
portrait painter, William Moore. His father taught him
to paint as a child but the family moved to London
after his father's death and he finished his education at
Kensington Grammar School. A member of the Royal
Academy from 1858, he travelled to France and Rome
in the pursuit of art. His earliest commissions included
designs for fabrics, wallpapers, tiles, murals and
stained glass which were all clearly influenced by Pre-
Raphaelite methods. Whistler admired Moore as a
great English artist and they met in 1865. This marked
a transition in Moore's style towards Oriental and
classical motifs, associated with the Aesthetic Movement. A bachelor throughout his life, Moore was elected
Associate of the Royal Society of Painters in 1884.

EVELYN DE MORGAN (1855-1919)

As the niece of Spencer Stanhope, one of the painters
selected by Rossetti to work on the Oxford Union
murals in 1857, Evelyn De Morgan inevitably became
a disciple of the Pre-Raphaelites. Although primarily
associated with the Aesthetic Movement, her myth-
ological subject matter and bright colouring draws
upon the Pre-Raphaelite imagination. From the age of
sixteen she attended the Slade School of Art and spent
some time with her uncle in Italy studying the work of
Michelangelo and the Italian mannerists. Under her
maiden name, Evelyn Pickering, she exhibited work

in 1877 and apart from her marriage to the potter, William De Morgan, in 1885, she scorned society for an unconventional career in art. According to an obituary of Evelyn De Morgan, penned by May Morris, she was dedicated to her work, painting from dawn until dusk every day for forty years.

DANTE GABRIEL ROSSETTI (1828-82)

The English-born son of an Italian political refugee, Rossetti's literary background is evident in his work as both poet and painter. Originally taught by John Sell Cotman, his drawing master, Rossetti took instruction in technique from Ford Maddox Brown, but felt repelled by formal rules and turned to Holman Hunt for more imaginative guidance. Rossetti's passion for literature led him to purchase a manuscript volume of William Blake's writing and drawing in 1847, and he was drawn to Holman Hunt in their student days at Oxford by a shared devotion to the poetry of John Keats. His association with Oxford continued in his work on the murals for the Union Debating Society with Morris and Burne-Jones.

Among other initiatives, Rossetti produced a literary periodical called *The Germ* in which he first published his poem *The Blessed Damozel* in 1850. The previous year he met Elizabeth Siddal, the beauteous milliner's assistant who set his genius alight. Although her own artistic talents were nurtured by Ruskin, her apotheosis came as one of the Pre-Raphaelite's most admired models. She first posed for Millais' *Ophelia*, spending the winter lying in a bath of cold water from which she contracted a severe chill, the start of ill-health that plagued her for the rest of her life. Rossetti painted her

the winter lying in a bath of cold water from which she
contracted a severe chill, the start of ill-health that
plagued her for the rest of her life. Rossetti painted her
relentlessly and despite a period of estrangement she
became his wife in 1860. It was an unhappy marriage;
Siddal was fiercely jealous and in fits of temper would
throw his paintings of other women from the window
of their Blackfriars' apartment into the Thames. The
couple had a stillborn child in 1861 and Siddal died the
following year from an overdose of laudanum.

Rossetti's creative powers diminished after the loss of
his muse and, grief-stricken, he tried to contact her
through seances. His imagination was only rekindled
through his love for Morris's wife, Jane Burden, the
pouting-lipped beauty who is often associated with his
art. Rossetti lived with William Morris and his wife at
Kelmscott Manor between1871-4. In 1870 he published
Poems, combining new verse written in praise of Jane
Burden with love poems he had buried with Siddal but
had exhumed from her coffin in 1869. Overwhelmed
with guilt over his adultery with Mrs Morris and
facing criticism of his *Poems*, he made an attempt at
suicide in 1872. It failed, but Rossetti became addicted
to chloral and he died a recluse in 1882.

FREDERICK SANDYS (1829-1904)

The son of a painter, Sandys was educated at the
Norwich School of Design. He began his career as a
portrait painter and antiquarian illustrator, exhibiting
at the Norwich Art Union even as a boy. He moved
to London in 1851 and worked as a draughtsman for
wood engravers. Sandys was one of a group of high-
calibre artists, known as the 'Illustrators of the 60s',

The sensual lines of his draughtsmanship and his
imaginative composition were translated by wood
engravers as a means of graphic reproduction. One of
his sketches, an amusing caricature of a painting by
Millais, so impressed Rossetti that he sought Sandys'
friendship and they lodged together at Rossetti's
Chelsea home in 1866. His carefree bohemian lifestyle
saddled him with endless debt. He abandoned his first
wife, had a brief fancy with a gypsy girl and a long-
term relationship with a young actress who bore him
nine children.

JOHN BYAM SHAW (1872-1919)

The son of a British civil servant, Shaw was born in India
but returned to England to be educated at St John's
Wood Art School. He graduated to the Royal Academy
Schools in 1890 and became the leading figure in a
London-based group of watercolourists, known as the
'label school' because of their characteristic signature
of a *trompe l'oeil* cartouche. The works he displayed
in an exhibition at the Royal Academy in 1898 saw a
revival of Pre-Raphaelite methods of observation and
vivacious colouring. Shaw was a prolific illustrator of
books and short stories and his work in this field
includes 39 volumes of Shakespeare. A dedicated art
teacher, in 1910 he founded the independent London
Art School that still bears his name.

SPENCER STANHOPE (1829-1908)

A pupil of George Frederic Watts, one of the last grand
allegorical history painters, Stanhope specialized
in classical work, making a close study of the Elgin
Marbles. As an undergraduate at Christ Church, Oxford,
he was involved with the decoration of the Oxford Union
debating hall, a year-long project led by Rossetti. The
Pre-Raphaelite style of his paintings and the allegorical
detail is echoed in the work of his niece, Evelyn De
Morgan. Due to ill-health, in 1872 Stanhope emigrated
to Italy and lived in the Villa Nuti on the outskirts of
Florence until his death.

JOHN MELHUISH STRUDWICK (1849-1937)

Strudwick began his artistic life in the early 1870s as
a studio-assistant to Burne-Jones. He exhibited chiefly
at the Grosvenor Gallery and was noted by George
Bernard Shaw who wrote an article about him which
appeared in the *Art Journal* in 1891. Strudwick enjoyed
the patronage of the wealthy shipowners William Imrie
and George Holt but his career sank into decline when
they withdrew their financial support. Strudwick
orchestrated his last exhibition to coincide with his
sixtieth birthday. His swan-song, *When Sorrow comes in
Summer Days, Roses Bloom in Vain*, was left deliberately
unfinished to reflect the disillusionment he felt at the
collapse of his career.

LIST OF PLATES

Edward Burne-Jones

Arthur in Avalon 1881-98
Oil on canvas
282 x 645.2 cm (whole panel)
Ponce, Puerto Rico,
Museo de Arte

Baleful Head, The 1886-7
Oil on canvas
155 x 130 cm
Stuttgart, Staatsgalerie

*Beatrice from Dante's
'Divine Comedy'* 1870
Gouache
66.7 x 48.9 cm
Private collection

Beguiling of Merlin, The 1874
Oil on canvas
186 x 111 cm
Port Sunlight,
Lady Lever Art Gallery

Garden Court, The 1873-90
Oil on canvas
125 x 231 cm (whole panel)
City of Bristol
Museum & Art Gallery

Garden of the Hesperides
1870-3
Gouache
119.4 x 97.8 cm
Private collection

Girl's Head 1858
Gouache and gold paint
on purple paper
34.3 x 24.1 cm
London, Hammersmith &
Fulham Libraries

Godhead Fires, The 1868-70
Oil on canvas
66 x 50.8 cm
Paris,
Joseph Setton Collection

Golden Stairs, The 1872-80
Oil on canvas
269.2 x 116.8 cm
London, Tate Gallery

Heart of the Rose, The 1901
Wool tapestry
155 x 201 cm
Private collection

*Last Sleep of Arthur in
Avalon, The* 1881-98
Oil on canvas
282 x 645.2 cm (whole panel)
Ponce, Puerto Rico,
Museo de Arte

Laus Veneris 1873-5
Oil on canvas
122 x 183 cm
Newcastle-upon-Tyne,
Laing Art Gallery

Mill, The 1882
Oil on canvas
91 x 198 cm
London,
Victoria & Albert Museum

Pan and Psyche 1869-74
Oil on canvas
65.1 x 54.3 cm
Cambridge, Massachusetts,
Fogg Art Gallery. Bequest of
Grenville L. Winthrop

Pilgrim at the Gate of Idleness
1874
Oil on canvas
97 x 131 cm
Private collection

*Portrait of La Baronne
Madeleine Deslandes*
Oil on canvas
116.2 x 58.4 cm
Private collection

Sleeping Beauty, The
from the *Briar Rose* series
1870-90
Oil on canvas
61 x 116.8 cm
Buscot, Oxon,
Faringdon Collection

Temperantia 1872
Watercolour
152.4 x 58.4 cm
Private collection

Three Graces, The c.1885
Pastel
135.9 x 69.9 cm
Carlisle
Museum & Art Gallery

Arthur Hughes

Ophelia 1852
Oil on canvas
68.6 x 123.8 cm (arched top)
Manchester City
Art Galleries

William Holman Hunt

Il Dolce Far Niente 1866
Oil on canvas
99.1 x 82.6 cm
New York,
Forbes Magazine Collection

John Everett Millais

Ophelia 1851-2
Oil on canvas
76.2 x 111.8 cm
London, Tate Gallery

'Yes or No?' 1871
Oil on canvas
112 x 86.5 cm
Private collection

Albert Joseph Moore

Apples 1875
Oil on canvas
29.2 x 50.8 cm
Private collection

Dreamers 1882
Oil on canvas
68.5 x 119.4 cm
Birmingham City
Museums & Art Gallery

Embroidery, An c.1881
Oil on canvas
32.5 x 11.5 cm
Private collection

Midsummer 1887
Oil on canvas
64 x 52.5 cm
Bournemouth,
Russell Cotes
Art Gallery & Museum

Evelyn De Morgan

Flora 1894
Oil on canvas
198 x 88.3 cm
London, Collection of the
De Morgan Foundation

*Hero Awaiting the Return
of Leander* 1885
Gouache on paper
laid on panel
57.8 x 29.2 cm
Private collection

Hope in the Prison of Despair
c.1887
Oil on panel
58.4 x 64.8 cm
Private collection

*Queen Eleanor and
Fair Rosamund* 1902
Oil on canvas
73.7 x 64.8 cm
London, Collection of the
De Morgan Foundation

Dante Gabriel Rossetti

Annie Miller 1860
Pen and ink on paper
25.5 x 24.2 cm
Manchester City
Art Galleries.
Courtesy of the Estate of
the late L.S. Lowry

Annie Miller c.1860
Pen and ink on paper
26.7 x 21.6 cm
Private collection

Artist's Wife, The 1860
Pencil on paper
25.8 x 25.2 cm
Cambridge,
Fitzwilliam Museum

Astarte Syriaca 1877
Oil on canvas
185 x 109 cm
Manchester City
Art Galleries

Beata Beatrix 1864
Oil on canvas
86.3 x 66 cm
London, Tate Gallery

Beata Beatrix 1872
Pastel
87 x 69 cm
Private collection

*Blessed Damozel, Study
for The* 1876
Chalk
54.9 x 56.5 cm
Manchester City
Art Galleries

Blessed Damozel, The 1875-8
Oil on canvas
174 x 94 cm
Port Sunlight,
Lady Lever Art Gallery

Bower Meadow, The 1872
Oil on canvas
86.3 x 68 cm
Manchester City
Art Galleries

Day Dream, The 1878
Pastel and black chalk
on paper
104.8 x 76.8 cm
Oxford,
Ashmolean Museum

Day Dream, The 1880
Oil on canvas
158.8 x 92.7 cm
London,
Victoria & Albert Museum

Donna della Fiamma, La 1870
Chalk
86.4 x 66 cm
Manchester City
Art Galleries

Elizabeth Siddal 1855
Pen and brown ink and
black ink on paper
12 x 11 cm
Oxford,
Ashmolean Museum

Ellen Smith 1867
Coloured chalks on
blue-grey paper
47.6 x 36.8 cm
London,
Victoria & Albert Museum

Ghirlandata, La 1873
Oil on canvas
115.6 x 87.6 cm
Corporation of London,
Guildhall Art Gallery

*Jane Burden,
later Mrs William Morris,
as Queen Guinevere* 1858
Ink, pencil and wash with
white highlights on paper
49.2 x 37.6 cm
Dublin,
National Gallery of Ireland

Joli Coeur 1867
Oil on panel
38.1 x 30.2 cm
Manchester City
Art Galleries

Lady of Pity, The 1870
Oil on canvas
85.1 x 72.4 cm
Bradford
Art Gallery & Museum

Mariana 1870
Oil on canvas
110.5 x 90.2 cm
City of Aberdeen
Art Gallery & Museums
Collection

May Morris 1872
Pastel
73.5 x 51 cm
Private collection

Monna Vanna 1866
Oil on canvas
88.9 x 86.4 cm
London, Tate Gallery

Mrs Beyer c.1862
Pen and ink, sepia and
brush on paper
16 x 18.9 cm
Cambridge,
Fitzwilliam Museum

Mrs Burne-Jones c.1860
Black chalk
26.7 x 32.6 cm
Private collection

Mrs William Morris 1865
Black chalk
41.5 x 33.9 cm
Private collection

Mrs William Morris 1873
Pen and ink and wash
22.4 x 17.8 cm
Private collection

Proserpine 1877
Oil on canvas
116.8 x 55.9 cm
London, Tate Gallery

Portrait of a Lady 1870
Chalk on paper
49.5 x 39.9 cm
Private collection

Reverie 1868
Coloured chalks on paper
83.8 x 71.1 cm
Oxford,
Ashmolean Museum

Study of a girl holding a leaf
Chalk
47 x 39.2 cm
Private collection

Venus Venticordia 1864-8
Oil on canvas
98.1 x 69.9 cm
Bournemouth,
Russell Cotes
Art Gallery & Museum

Frederick Sandys

Love's Shadow 1867
Oil on panel
40.6 x 32.4 cm
New York,
Forbes Magazine Collection

Oriana 1861
Oil on panel
25.4 x 20.3 cm
London, Tate Gallery

Portrait of Mary Sandys 1871
Chalk
52.1 x 40.6 cm
Private collection

Proud Maisie 1867
Black and red chalks
36.8 x 27.6 cm
London,
Victoria & Albert Museum

Proud Maisie c.1903
Pencil and crayon
39.4 x 30.1 cm
London,
Victoria & Albert Museum

Red Cap, The 1900
Coloured chalks
50 x 32 cm
Private collection

Vivien 1863
Oil on canvas
64 x 52.5 cm
Manchester City
Art Galleries

John Byam Shaw

Blessed Damozel, The 1895
Oil on canvas
94 x 180.4 cm
Corporation of London,
Guildhall Art Gallery

Spencer Stanhope

Love and the Maiden 1877
Oil on canvas
138.5 x 202.5 cm
Private collection

Penelope c.1864
Oil on canvas
106 x 80 cm
London, Collection of the
De Morgan Foundation

John Melhuish Strudwick

Symphony, A 1903
Oil on canvas
114.3 x 67.3 cm
Private collection

*When Sorrow Comes in
Summer Days, Roses Bloom
in Vain* 1859
Oil on canvas
88.9 x 54 cm
Private collection

PHOTOGRAPHIC ACKNOWLEDGEMENTS

City of Aberdeen Art Gallery & Museums
Ashmolean Museum, Oxford
The Bridgeman Art Library, London
BAL/Agnew & Sons, London
BAL/Birmingham City Museums & Art Gallery
BAL/Bradford Art Gallery & Museum
BAL/City of Bristol Museum & Art Gallery
BAL/Carlisle Museum & Art Gallery, Cumbria
BAL/Christie's, London
BAL/Russell Cotes Art Gallery & Museum, Bournemouth
BAL/Anthony Crane Collection
BAL/Forbes Magazine Collection, New York
BAL/Faringdon Collection, Buscot, Oxon
BAL/The Fine Art Society, London
Fine Art Photographs
Fitzwilliam Museum, Cambridge
BAL/Guildhall Art Gallery, Corporation of London
BAL/Hammersmith & Fulham Libraries, London
BAL/Laing Art Gallery, Newcastle-upon-Tyne
BAL/Lady Lever Art Gallery, Port Sunlight
BAL/Manchester City Art Galleries
    Courtesy of the Estate of the late L.S. Lowry
BAL/Roy Miles Gallery, 29 Bruton Street, London W1
BAL/The De Morgan Foundation, London
BAL/Museo de Arte, Ponce, Puerto Rico
National Gallery of Ireland, Dublin
National Museums & Galleries on Merseyside
    Lady Lever Art Gallery, Port Sunlight
BAL/Joseph Setton Collection, Paris
BAL/Staatsgalerie, Stuttgart
BAL/Tate Gallery, London
BAL/Victoria & Albert Museum, London

BAL = The Bridgeman Art Library, London

Phaidon Press Limited
Regent's Wharf
All Saints Street
London N1 9PA

First published 1994
Reprinted 1996, 1997, 1999
© 1994 Phaidon Press Limited

ISBN 0 7148 3252 9

A CIP catalogue record for this book
is available from the British Library.

Printed in Hong Kong